I0709690

Done Doing Time is dedicated to Concetta Harris and Linda Todd.

Their strength, courage, and love drive them to succeed and
be beacons of light to their families and friends. I am deeply indebted
to both women for their openness and willingness to make
Done Doing Time a reality for all of us.

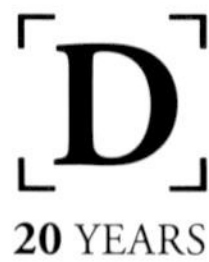

20 YEARS

Cofounders: Taj Forer and Michael Itkoff
Creative Director: Ursula Damm
Copy Editor: Gabrielle Fastman

ISBN: 978-1-954119-20-8
Library of Congress Control Number: 2023931541

Printed by Ofset Yapimevi, Turkey

Daylight Books
E-mail: info@daylightbooks.org
Web: www.daylightbooks.org

DONE DOING TIME A PORTRAIT OF LIFE AFTER PRISON

Hinda Schuman

Daylight

FINDING LINDA AND CONCETTA

Hinda Schuman

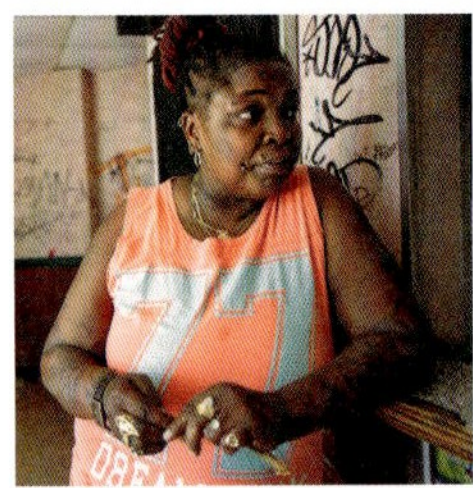

Concetta Harris

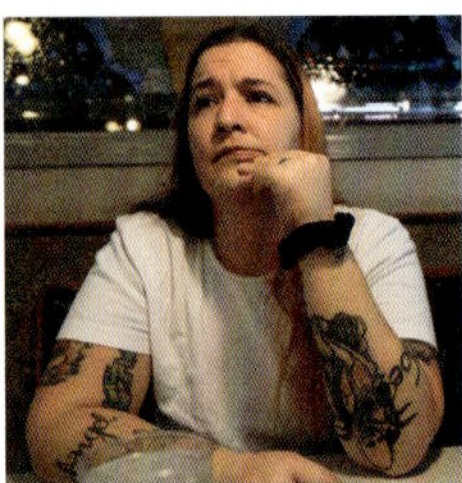

Linda Todd

In 2006 I was invited to attend the graduation event for the women of New Directions for Women. NDFW was an alternative-to-incarceration program located in the Germantown neighborhood of Philadelphia, where I also live. I was very moved by the short speeches given by the women who spoke of their year at NDFW, their previous years spent in prisons in Pennsylvania, and what turns in life got them into the prisons. I made a note to myself that, if or when I had time, this would be a place I would like to volunteer.

Be careful what you wish for.

In 2007 I was laid off from the *Philadelphia Inquirer*, where I had worked for twenty years as a photojournalist.

In 2009 I found myself at New Directions for Women in a basement room, with long tables, folding chairs, and green walls. Around the table were about fourteen women, all of whom wished they were upstairs where the TV had afternoon soap operas playing. Maybe they wished they were in their rooms napping. But here we were, and it was up to me to provide enlightenment.

I have a history of people coming to me from the "bad bench." From 1971 until 1978 I was a teacher in Bellows Falls, Vermont. I was running a special classroom in an unused locker room in the basement of the middle school. There, students were sent to me from the classrooms they had been kicked out of. My career became one of working with the students normally spending their days on the "bad bench" in the principal's office. It was a mutual attraction between the bad kids and me.

Not too big a stretch to see myself happy in a crowd of ex-felons. Every week when I arrived at NDFW, I brought a bag of fresh fruit. The women ate the grapes and oranges and I read aloud from

The Diary of Anne Frank, Three Cups of Tea, and *Alice in Wonderland.* We did word and number puzzles and learned to read a map. One day I approached the director of NDFW and asked if I could make photographs there. Then I asked the women and they agreed. Twice a year we did formal portraits so they could send home photographs of themselves to family to show how good they looked now. I was allowed to come and go and join in as I pleased. I stayed for dinner, watched while they scrubbed the floors and walls. I joined in my first NA and AA meetings. As Myra said to me, "You know, Miss Hinda, if you just got arrested, you could move in here."

Linda graduated in late 2009. Her addiction was gone. During her time at NDFW she was awarded all sorts of privileges because she worked hard, got a job, and commuted to the work site and back faithfully. Such a hard worker too; everyone wanted Linda on the job. We kept in touch. Until she disappeared. She was not answering her phone.

Concetta arrived in 2010. Concetta could sew and fix bicycles. I drove her to her first apartment, with her son carrying the sewing machine. She settled in, her younger daughter sometimes on the couch, her son sometimes bringing his son for a visit. And then Concetta disappeared too. Adriana, her younger daughter, took me with her to visit Concetta at Riverside Correctional Facility.

Linda called. She was out of jail. She says she was in the car when her brother committed a robbery. Back and forth; in and out. We stayed in touch as we could.

But then, in 2018, Concetta was in her own apartment on Erie Avenue and Linda was living with her stepmother in the Kensington neighborhood. I was happy to see their new resolve to keep clean and work hard and stay out of prison. Linda worked at a diner in the heart of the heroin and opioid drug trade in Philadelphia. Every day (and she worked seven days a week) she walked past the swaying shells of people, the dropped needles, and the offers to buy. She kept walking. Concetta made places in her small apartment for her two daughters and granddaughter: Shakira on the floor, Concetta on the couch, and Adriana and the infant Brielle in the bedroom. It was family life: TV shows, laundromat trips, getting meals together. Concetta was an anchor to her children and the neighborhood. Linda worked at the diner and was trying to get her mother and brother off heroin, while keeping herself safe and busy.

I went to the diner to see Linda at work and visited her at her stepmother Catherine's. Linda's mother, Maryann, lived there too for a while, along with Catherine's daughter, son-in-law, and grandson. I went shopping with Concetta for food and went along to the laundromat. I met her friends at outdoor barbecues, which she hosted for the neighborhood. At first people were a bit suspicious of me, and why not? I had a big camera. But Linda and Concetta both made it clear that I was OK. I could be trusted. And I brought photographs for all, and the pictures were free.

It's 2022 now. Concetta has decided the quiet life is best. She isn't out on the streets much after dark. She has a new boyfriend with a steady job. She needs some knee surgery but has put that off, since Covid is an issue and her diabetes has kept her from being cleared for surgery.

Linda has moved twice, each time further from the epicenter of the drug crisis. She and her boyfriend, Karlos, have a rented house that is clearly a home. Sometimes she and Karlos are together and sometimes not. Linda started a lawn-care business while working steadily as an aide for a woman with dementia. She was laid off from the health-aide job during the Covid pandemic. She then was hired at a pizza takeout restaurant, got a catering job, and is now an assistant manager at Primo's, a sandwich chain.

Since the pandemic, my image making has tapered. In 2022 I photographed Concetta's fifty-first birthday party. And sadly, I attended the funeral for Linda's mother and photographed at the graveside.

Concetta and Linda are two amazing women whom I feel honored and delighted to have as strong connections in my life. Concetta calls me her "white mom," which I find endearing. We keep in touch via text messages and phone calls and occasional visits. I love them both.

Postscript

Today is October 11, 2022. This is day two of Linda's recovery from using crack cocaine. She said, "Put this in the book." People relapse and recover again. They regain their footing and keep on fighting to live their lives with dignity and purpose. Why or how did she start using again? We sat on her porch in the fall sunshine, and she told me just how prevalent the drugs are, and how tempting it is to fall back into the pattern of fighting off grief and frustration and feeling abandoned by others by turning to drugs, which make everything seem OK. She will find her way back to where she wants to be. It's another in a long series of hurdles for her to leap over and land squarely on her feet.

Concetta has been dealing with a landlord who is trying to evict her for nonpayment of her rent. But Concetta has receipts and I have written to a lawyer on her behalf. It's very unsettling to be threatened with eviction, especially falsely. But she is strong and is keeping her life together. Her boyfriend, Lou, began using cocaine, so she told him to leave.

Concetta and her previous boyfriend Kareem are back together again. He is the one who appears with her frequently throughout the book. Shakira, Concetta's older daughter, has been living with her and is due to start a job at Amazon later this month. She has passed her drug test. Adriana, Concetta's younger daughter, is expecting a boy in February. This is her third child, and the family is very excited to meet the newest family member.

A MIRROR IN THE PHOTOGRAPH

Magdalena Solé

Hinda's photographs transcend the commonplace. They dance, collide, are in your face with an unapologetic candor and directness. They electrify, as do her subjects, who allow her to bring their lives, their joy and suffering in front of her camera. It is Hinda's unique talent to find people on the "bad bench," as she calls it. She connects, teaches, extends a hand, listens, and befriends.

Hinda is a child of an immigrant Jewish mother who was sent in 1922, at the age of six, by boat from Poland to live with a distant and unknown relative in Tennessee. Hinda's mother, Sonia, had to rely on her own intelligence and skills to survive. Hinda instinctively finds people who also know how to turn tragedy into opportunity, despair into strength. Linda and Concetta, the two protagonists in this book, managed to extract themselves from a life in and out of prison, and against all odds are on the road to recovery and becoming the people they want to be.

Hinda is a storyteller; her language is the photographs she renders with precision and dedication. Her stories are the lives of people she deeply cares about. Hinda doesn't look away.

Hinda never averts her eyes when others do. Where others place judgment and blame on convicts or other marginalized people, Hinda does not. She simply tries to help. She is one of those rare people who cares fearlessly. When someone is in need, she moves toward them, attracted like a moth to light. This caring is the thread in her photography.

Like Linda and Concetta, Hinda reinvented herself, coming out as a lesbian at a time when it was considered taboo or worse, never flinching. She moved to Philadelphia to attend art school, when repairing old chicken coops in Vermont no longer held the romance it once did. She lost her job as a photojournalist after twenty years, when newspapers decided photography was no longer a valuable asset, and became the photographer she wanted to be.

I know little about incarceration except for an experience I had that coincided with 9/11. I was filming at the notorious New York City prison of Rikers Island when the World Trade Center collapsed, and I experienced both a lockdown and the wrath of thousands of prisoners chanting, "Burn Rikers." The film crew and I managed to flee unscathed, crossing the one bridge that connected the prison to the rest of the city.

A bridge in mysticism is known to connect two realms of existence; a passage to another reality was never more palatable than on that day.

Concetta and Linda, although at a different prison, crossed that bridge between freedom and incarceration several times. Stepping from the realm of freedom to a place where people are subjected to rage, cruelty, and threats conveyed by simple glances. A place where even sounds are menacing and sharp. Shedding that experience is not for the faint of heart. Remembering that day at Rikers, I think of Linda and Concetta and how they might have overcome that life in prison.

Hinda practices the "long form" of documentary, a dying genre, at a time when people prefer to "grab" pictures and then move on. The long form requires years of letting the images unfold; it also requires the photographer to become immersed in the lives of the people they photograph. Hinda has known Linda Todd since 2009 and Concetta Harris since 2010.

The camera affords the photographer the opportunity to meet people they wouldn't have met otherwise. It is also a bridge to other realms. It lets us connect with strangers and find the familiar in the unfamiliar. It reveals the joy of knowing that beauty can be found in the most unexpected places. Hinda's camera is her dowsing rod. I have been so fortunate to know her and her uncanny talent to create art in the everyday.

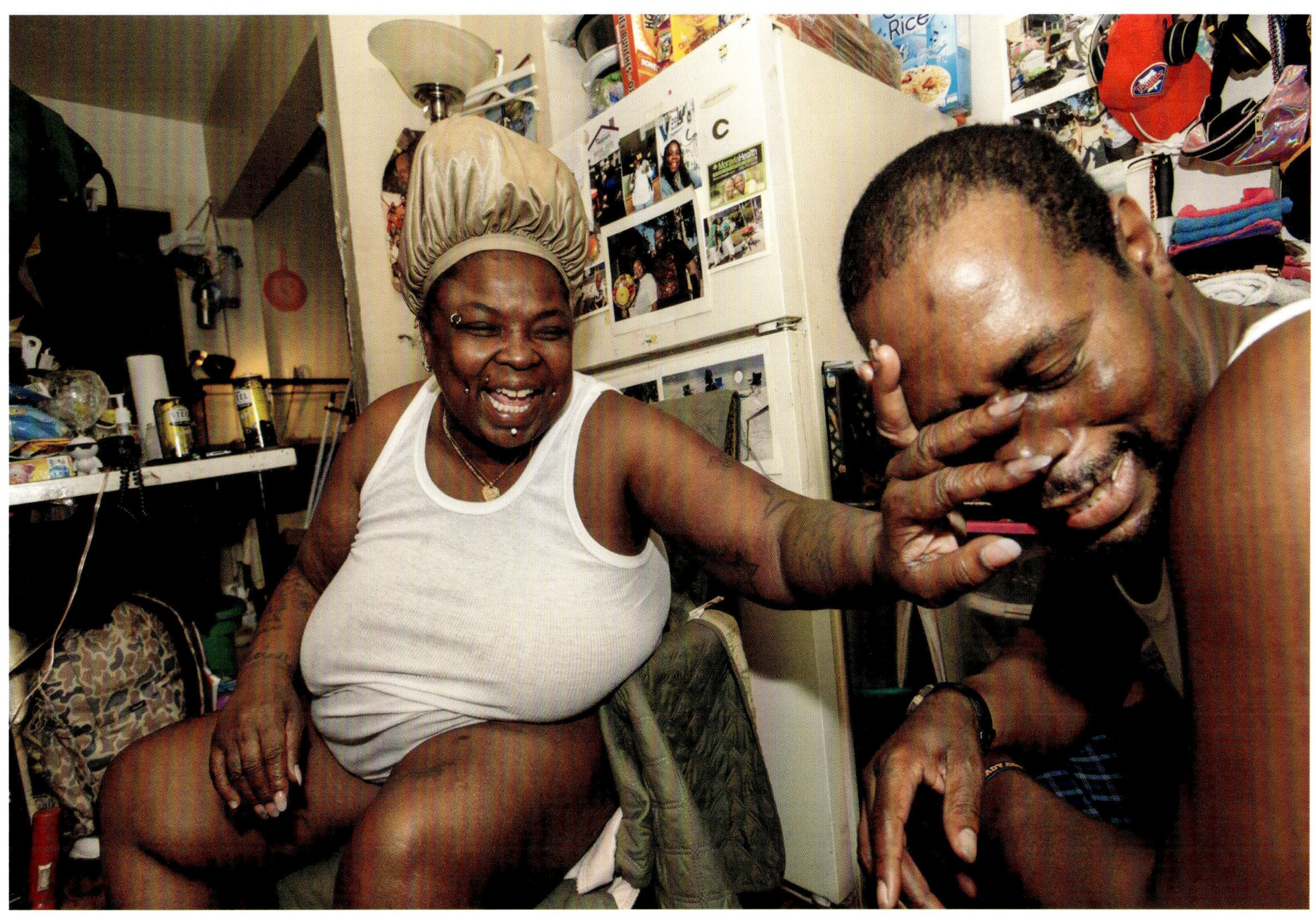

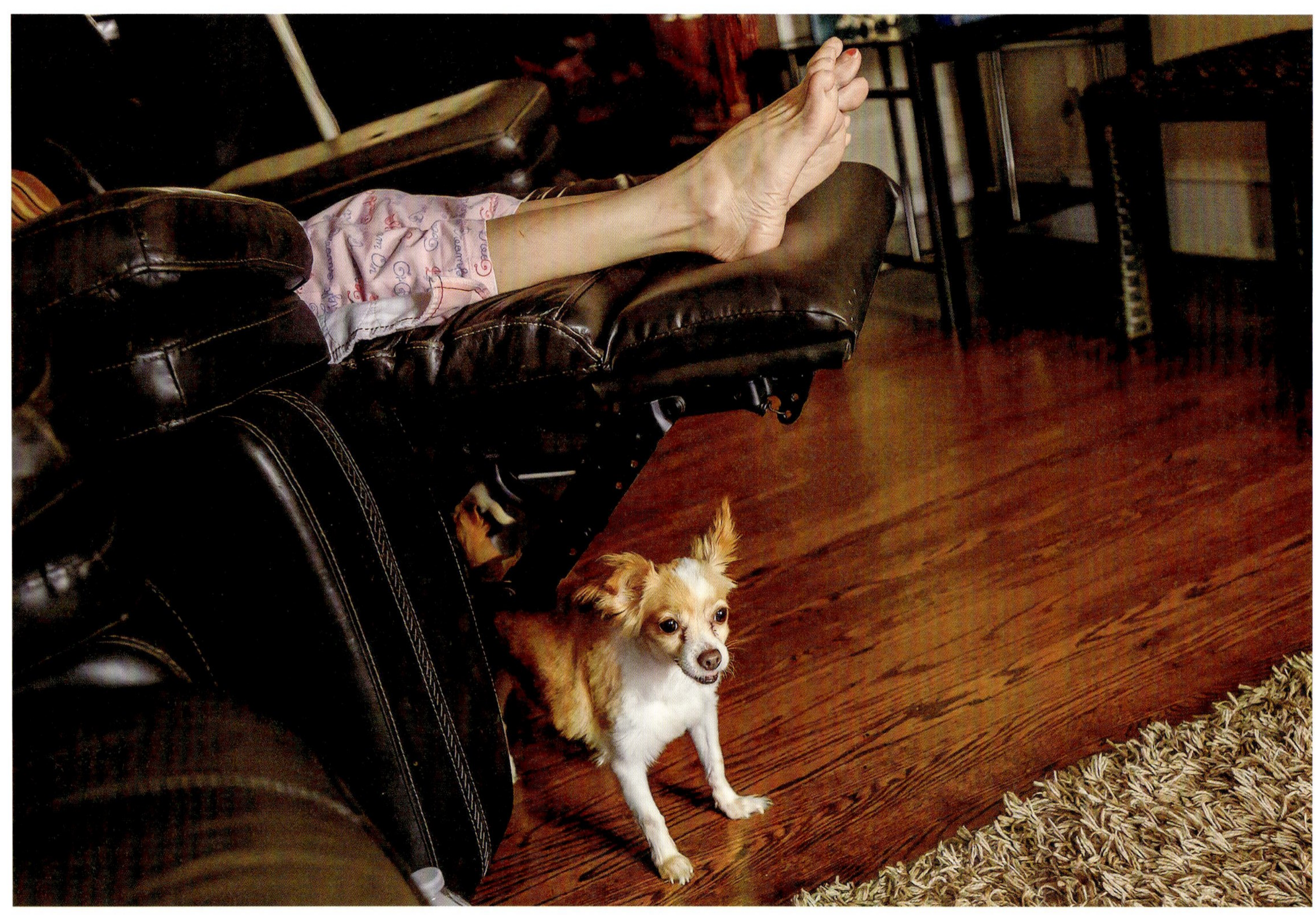

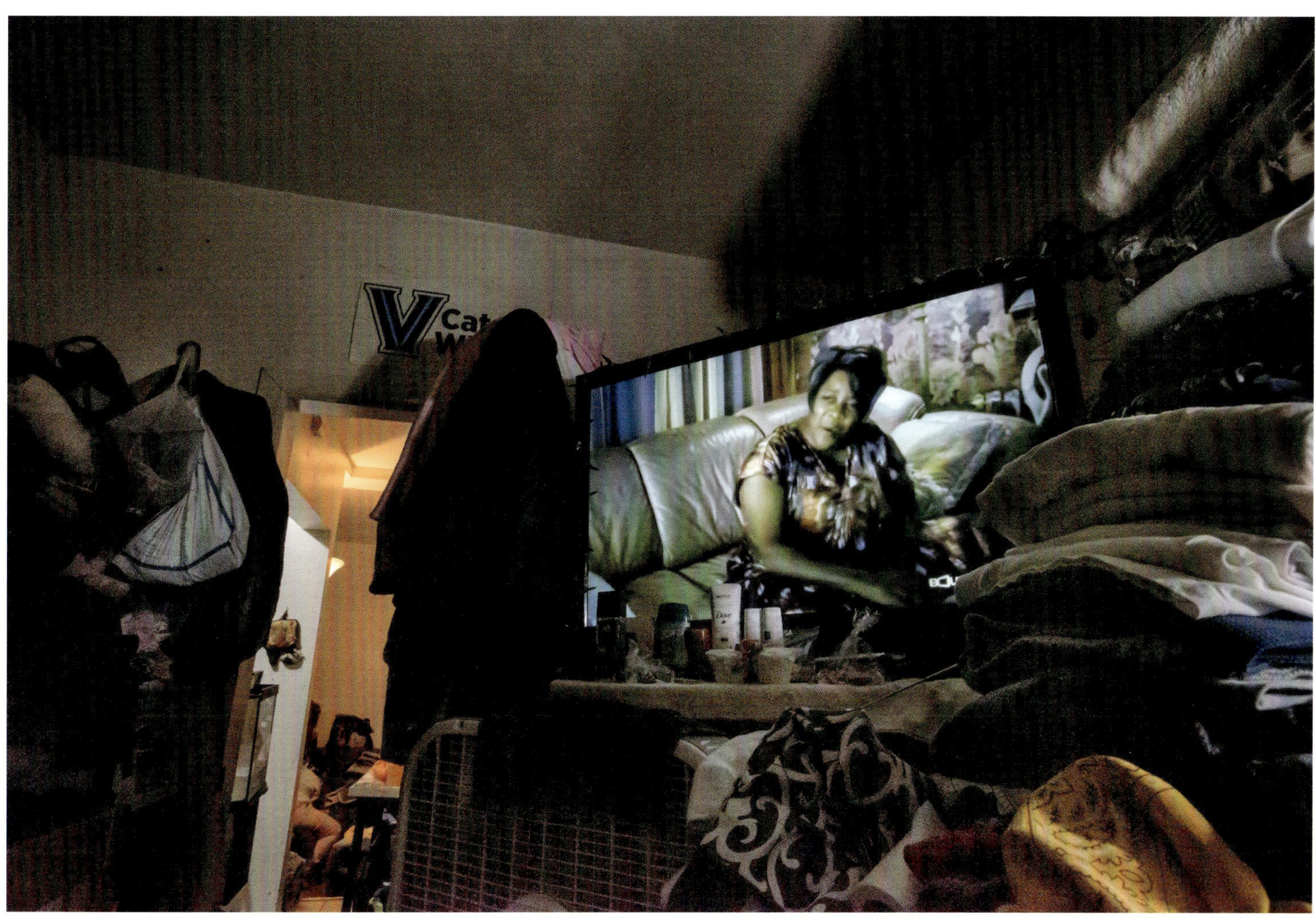

V
Cat
W

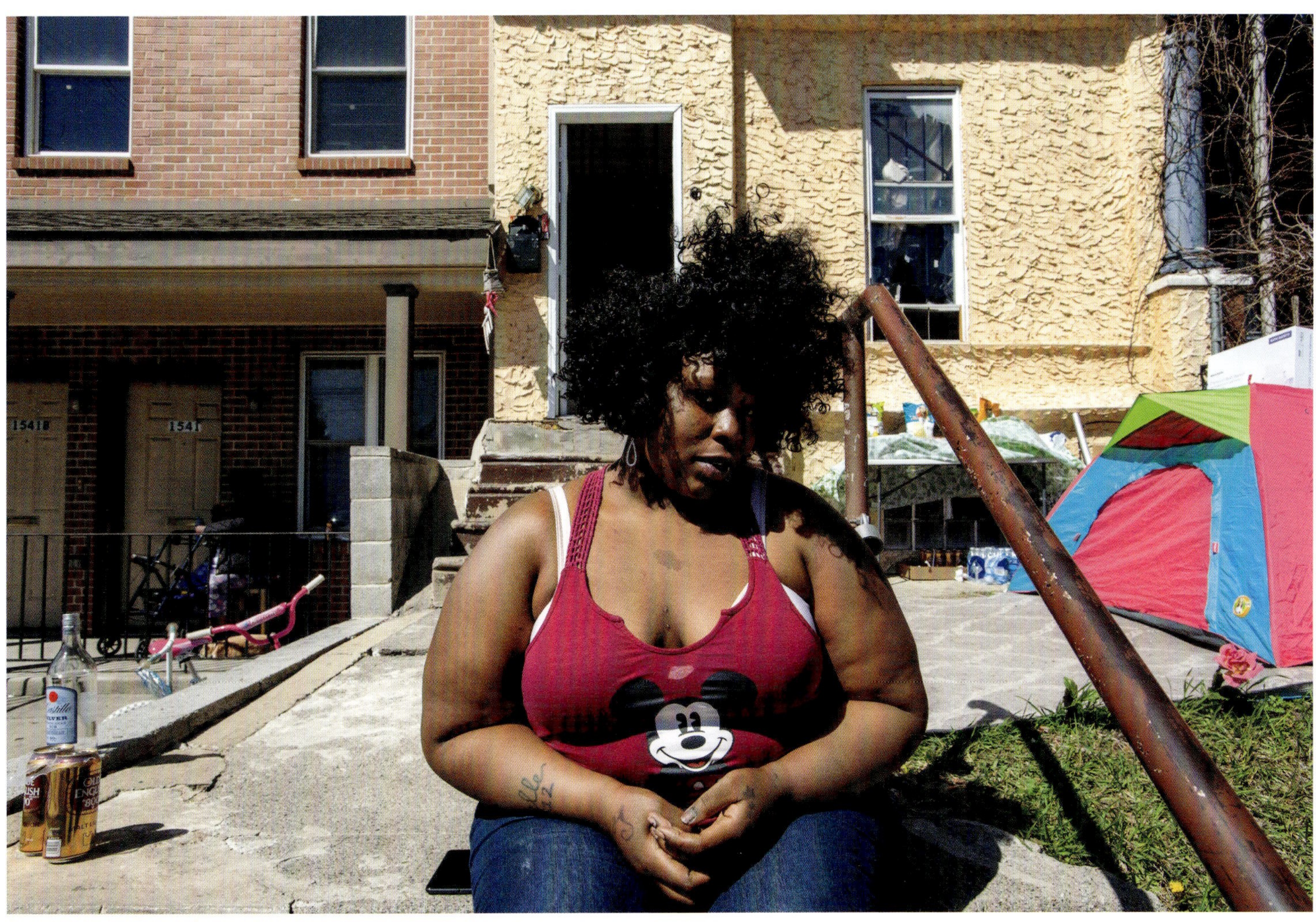

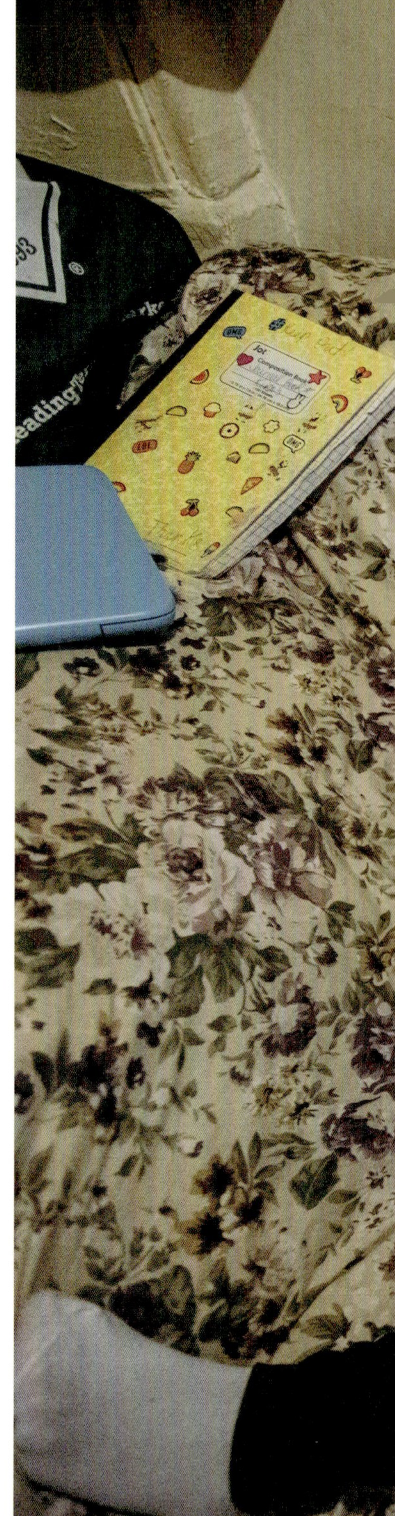

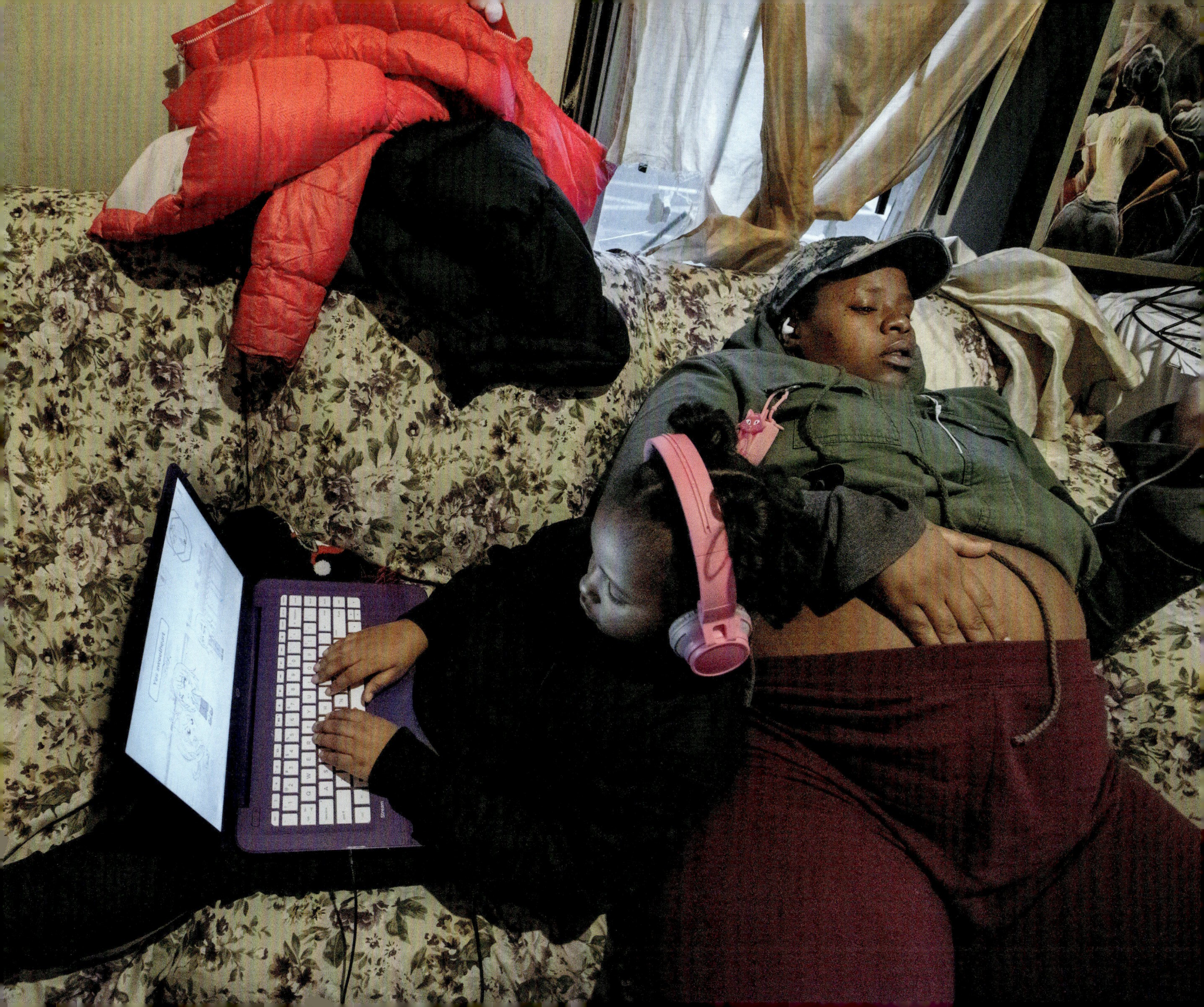

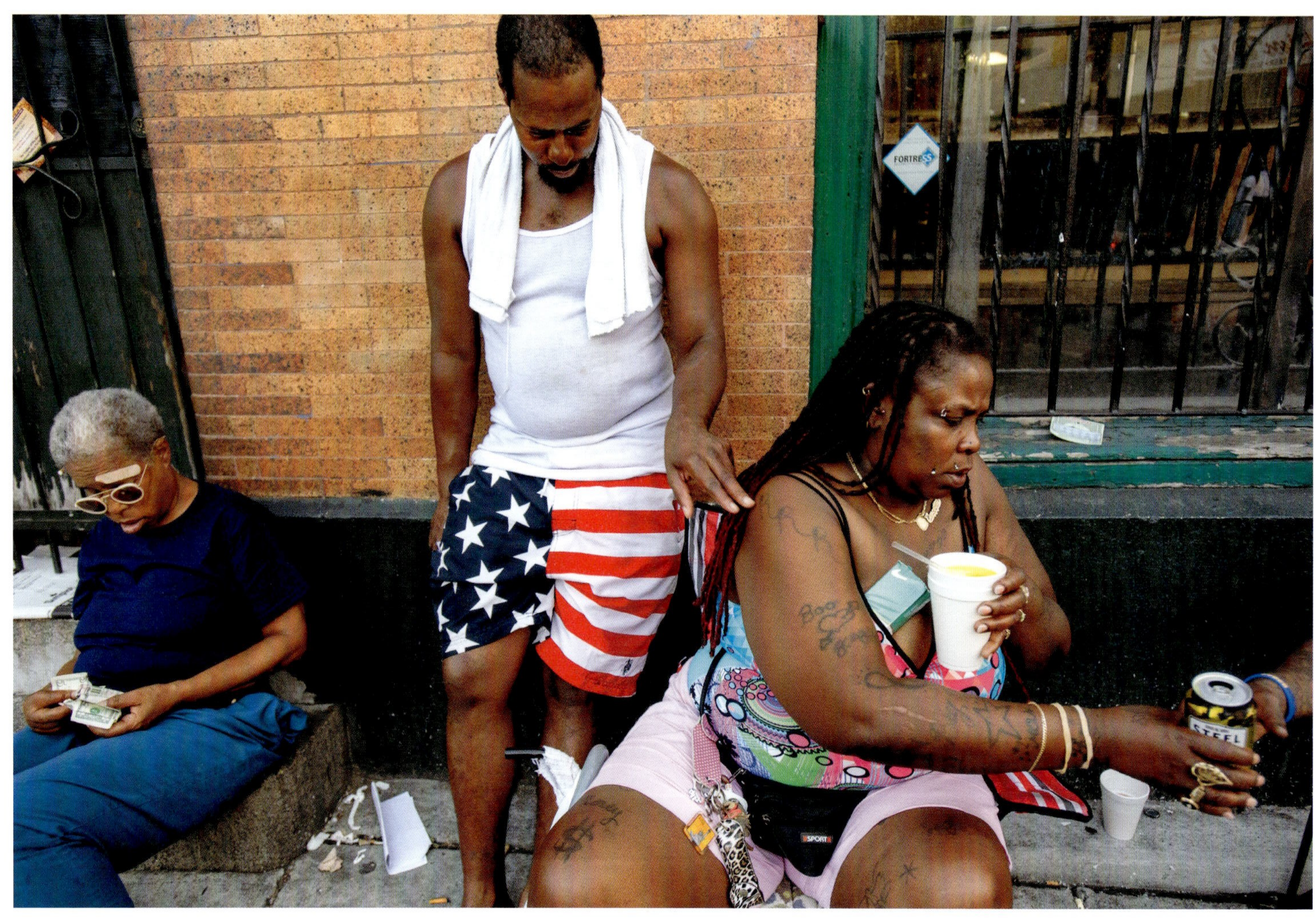

"I sent him home. I don't need his sorry ass. I pay all the bills. I do everything.
I got people that love me now."

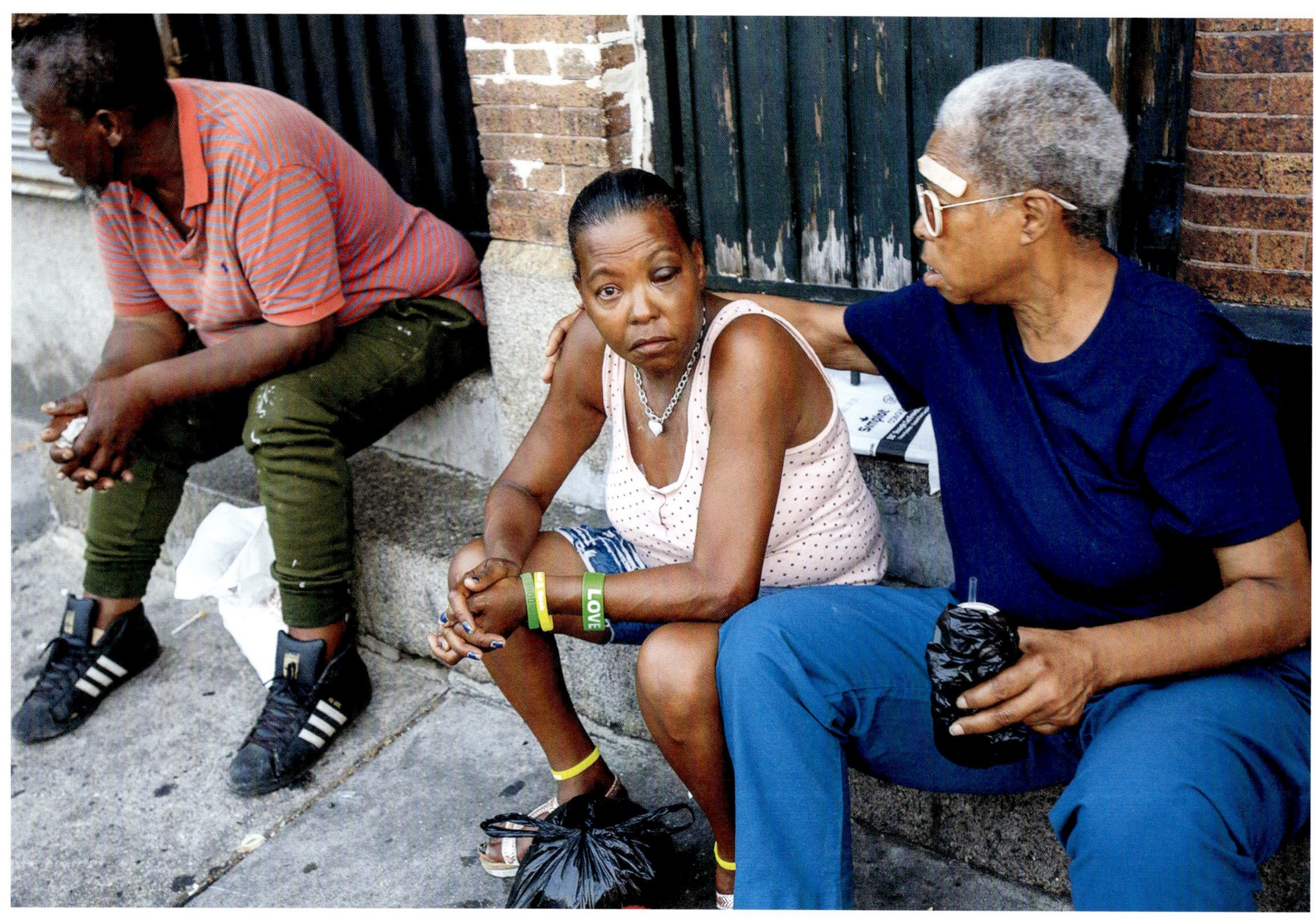

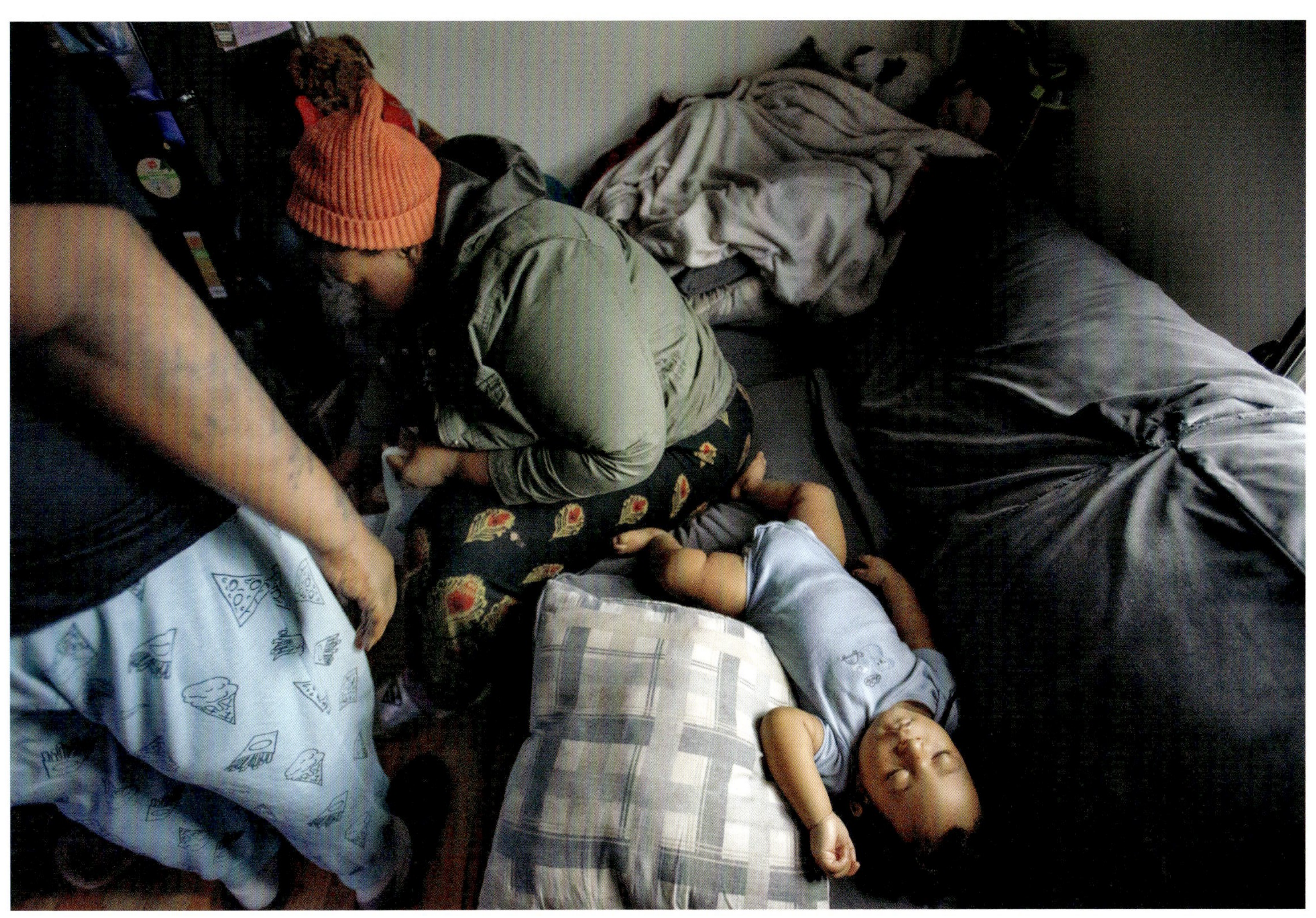

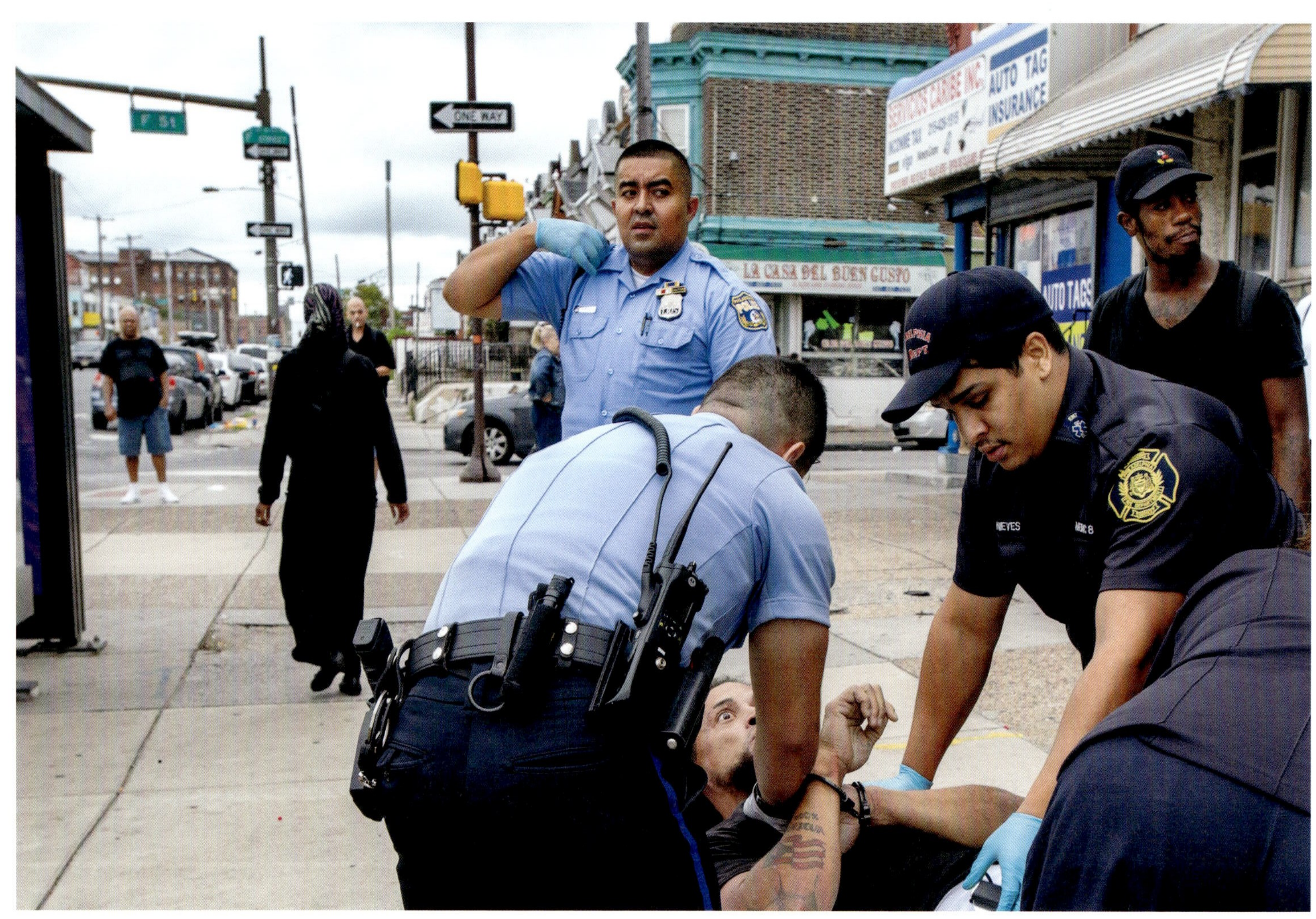

ONE WAY
F St
SERVICIOS CARIBE INC.
AUTO TAG INSURANCE
LA CASA DEL BUEN GUSTO
AUTO TAGS
NIEVES

"I am not going back to that life."

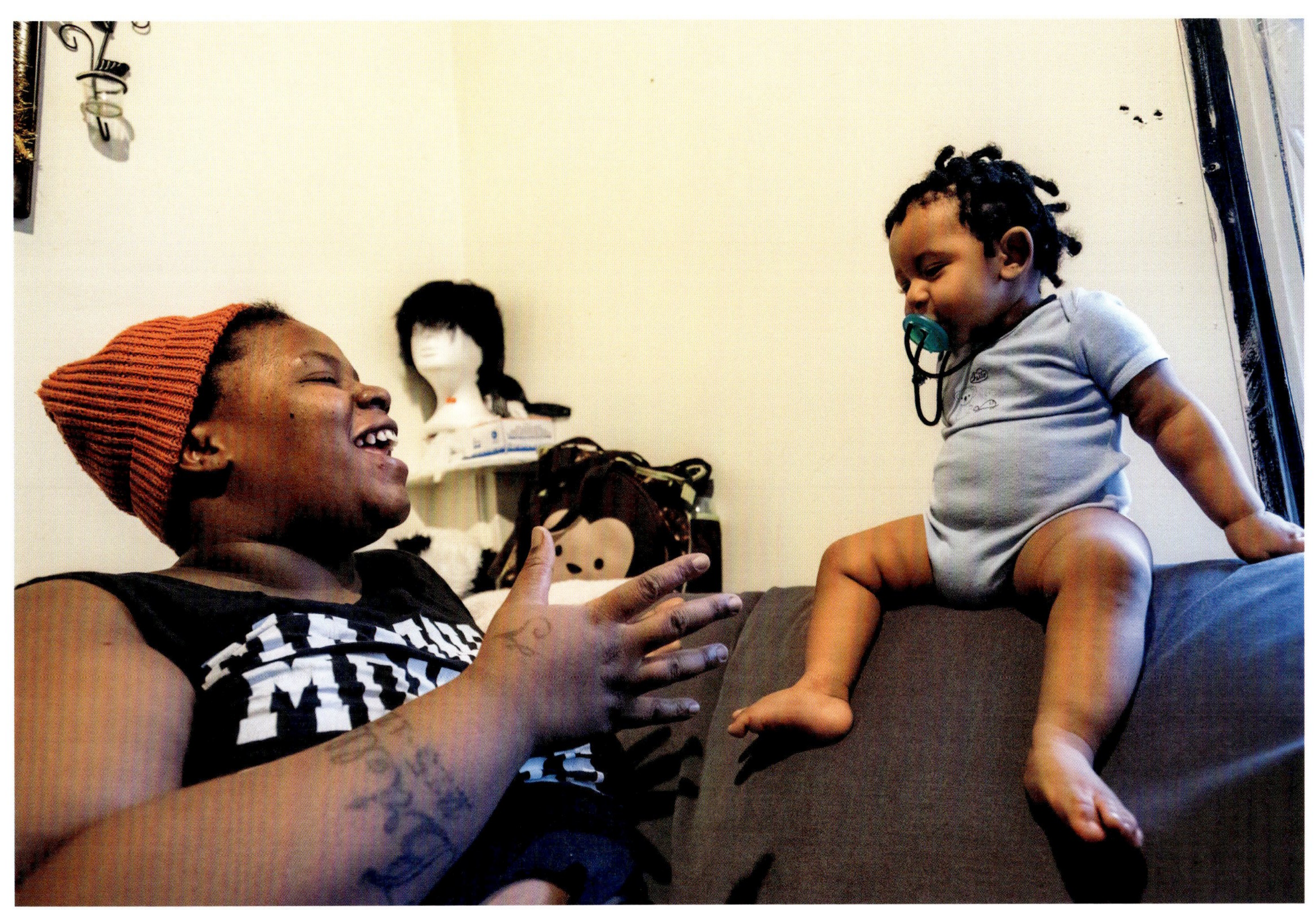

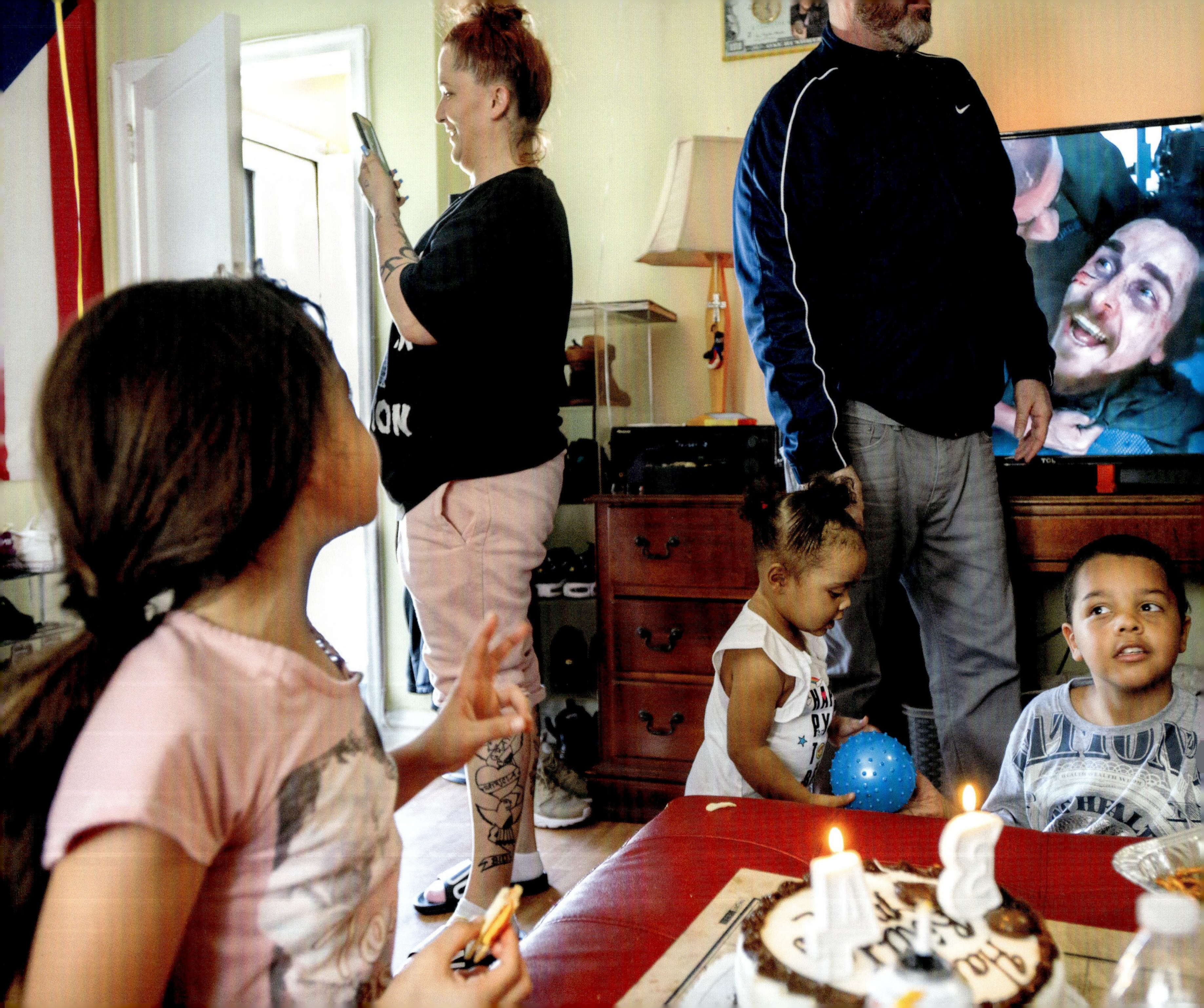

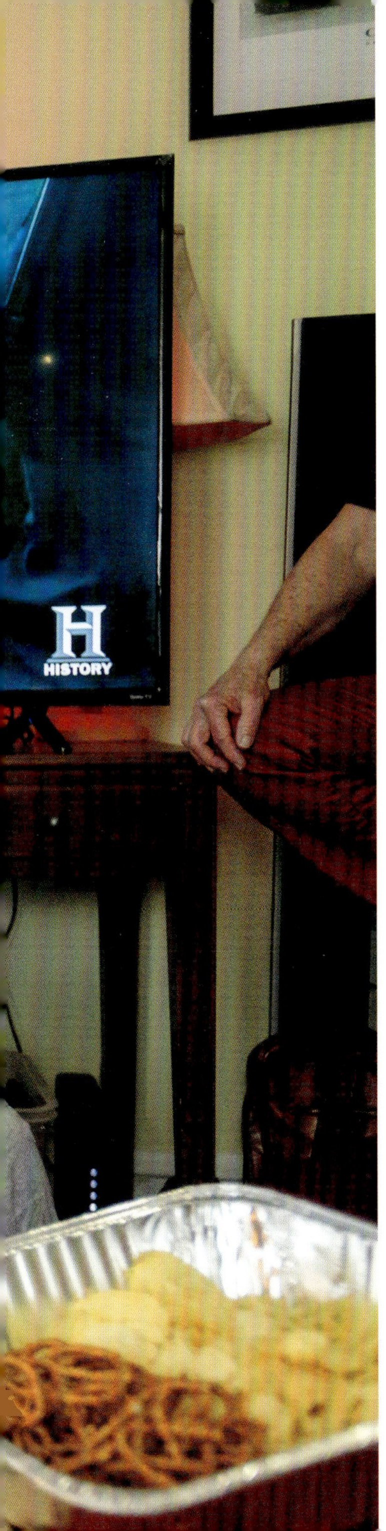

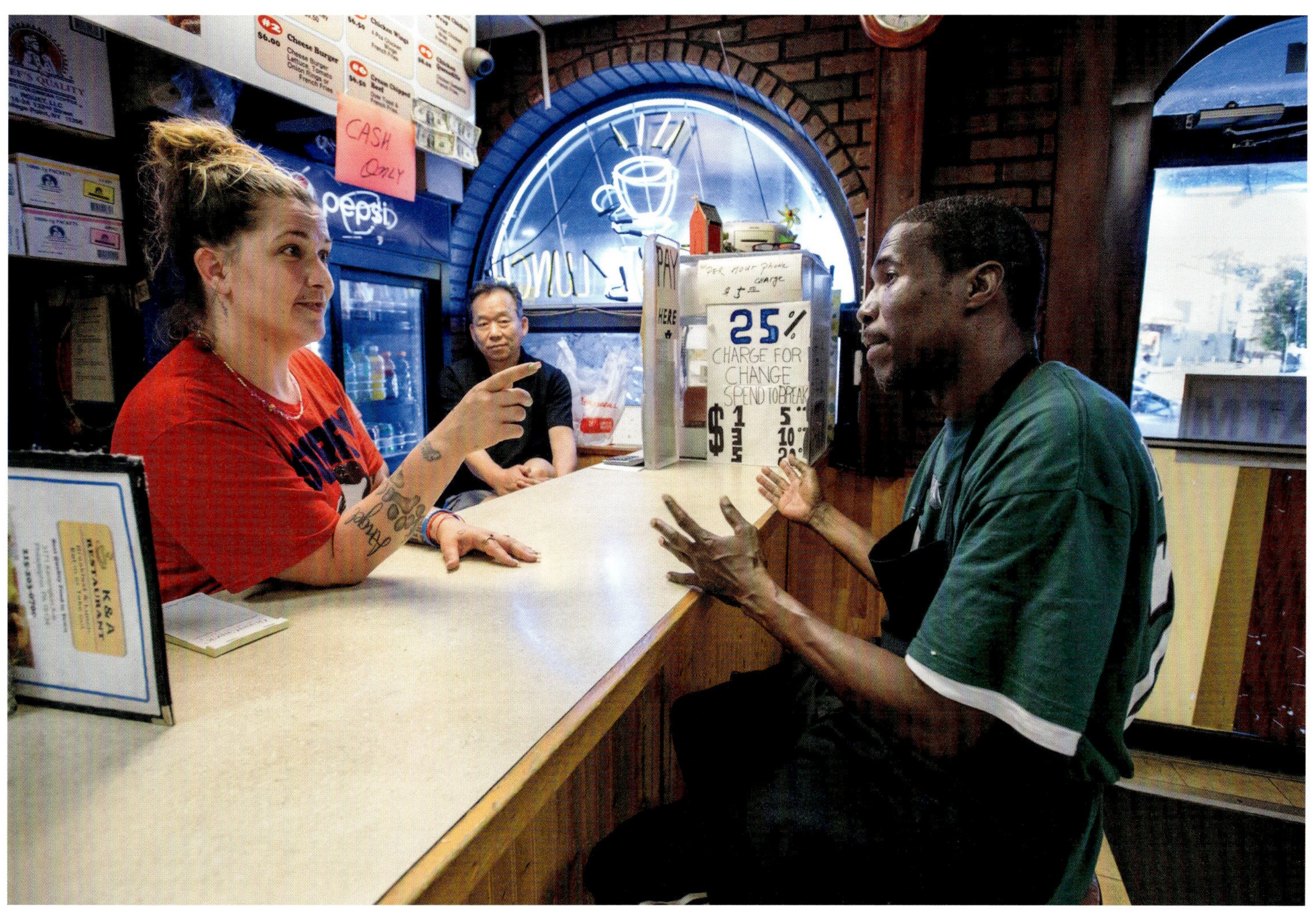
CASH Only
Pepsi
PER HOUR PHONE
charge
25%
CHARGE FOR
CHANGE
SPEND TO BREAK
$1
5
10
2
K&A
RESTAURANT

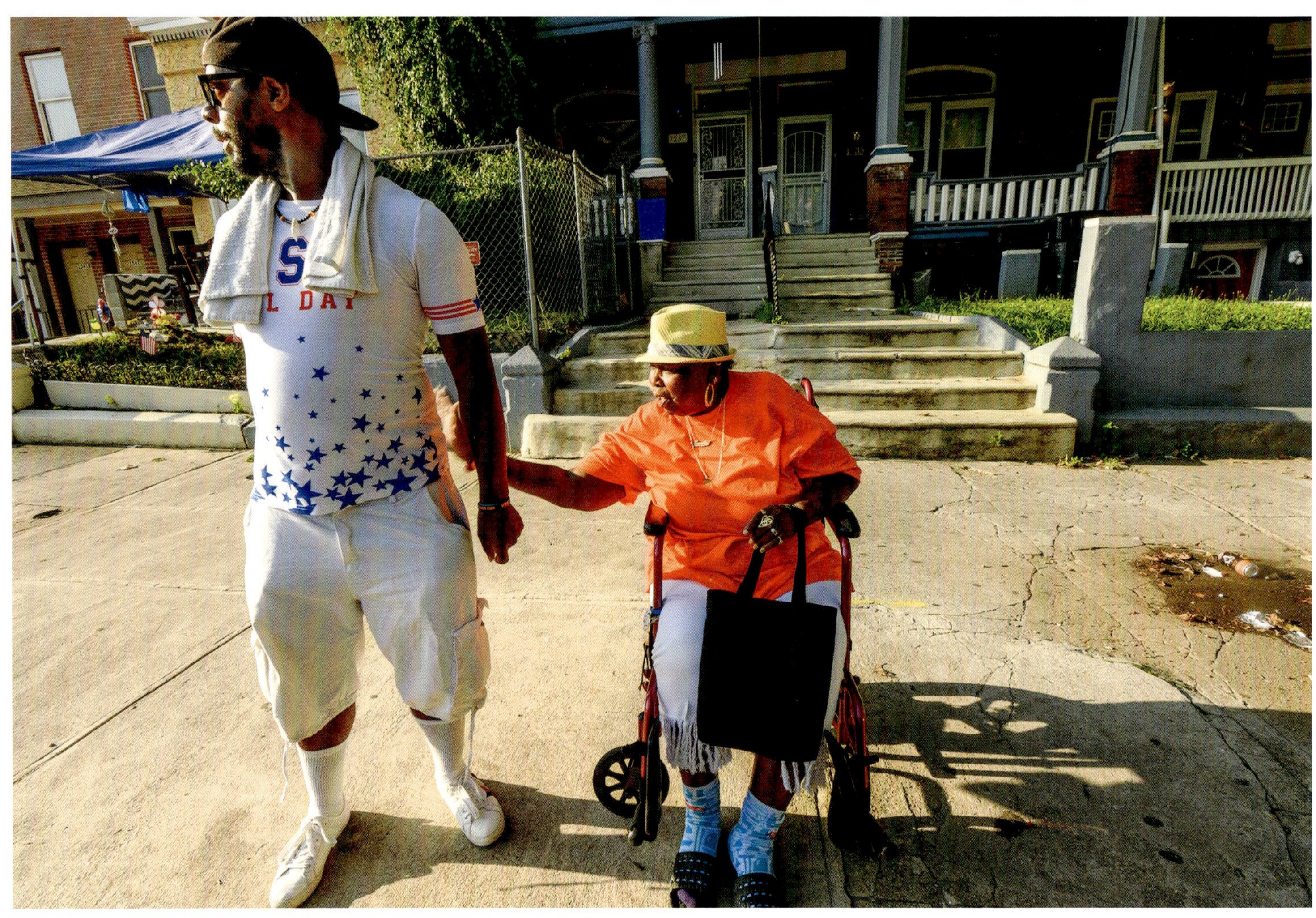

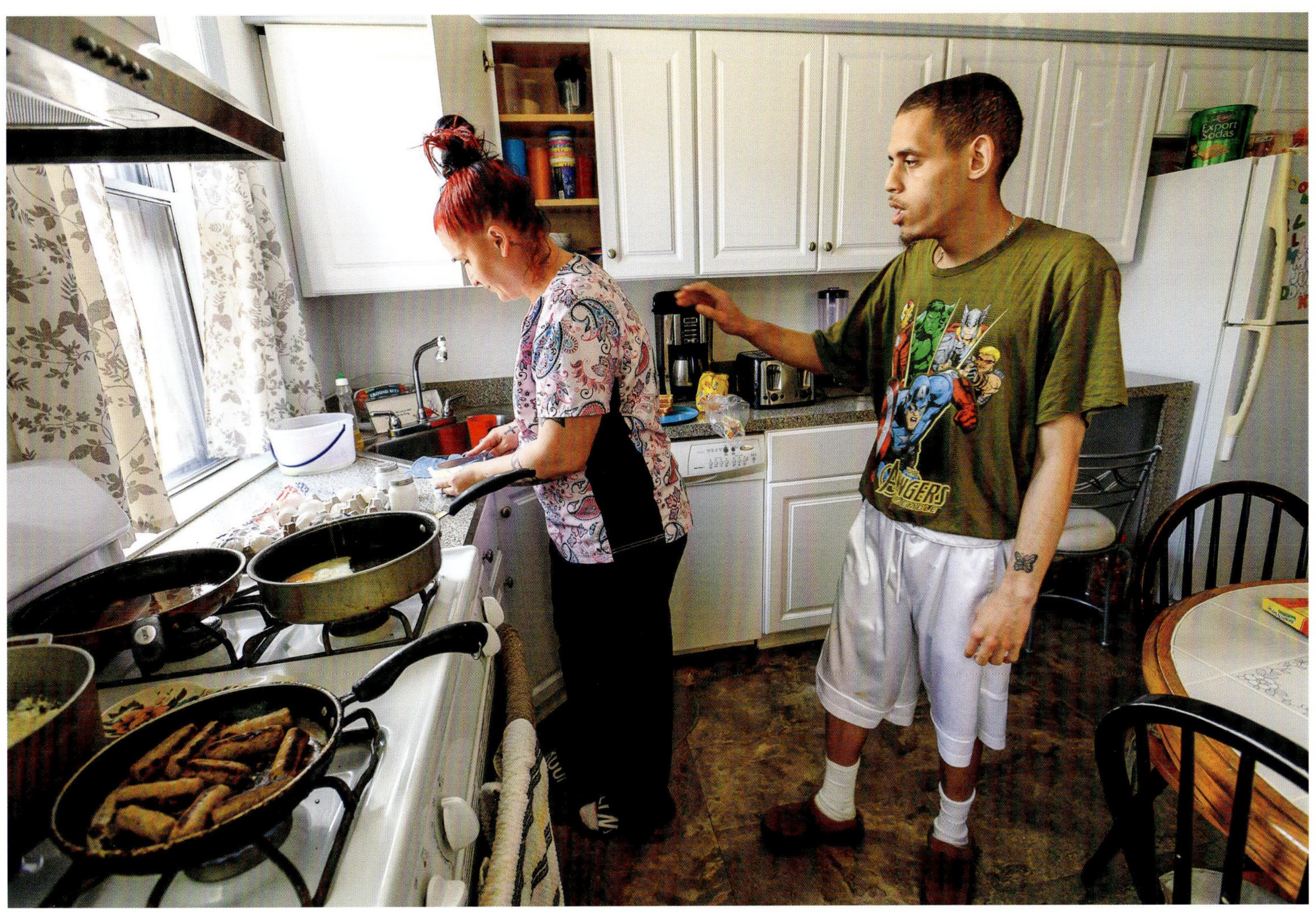

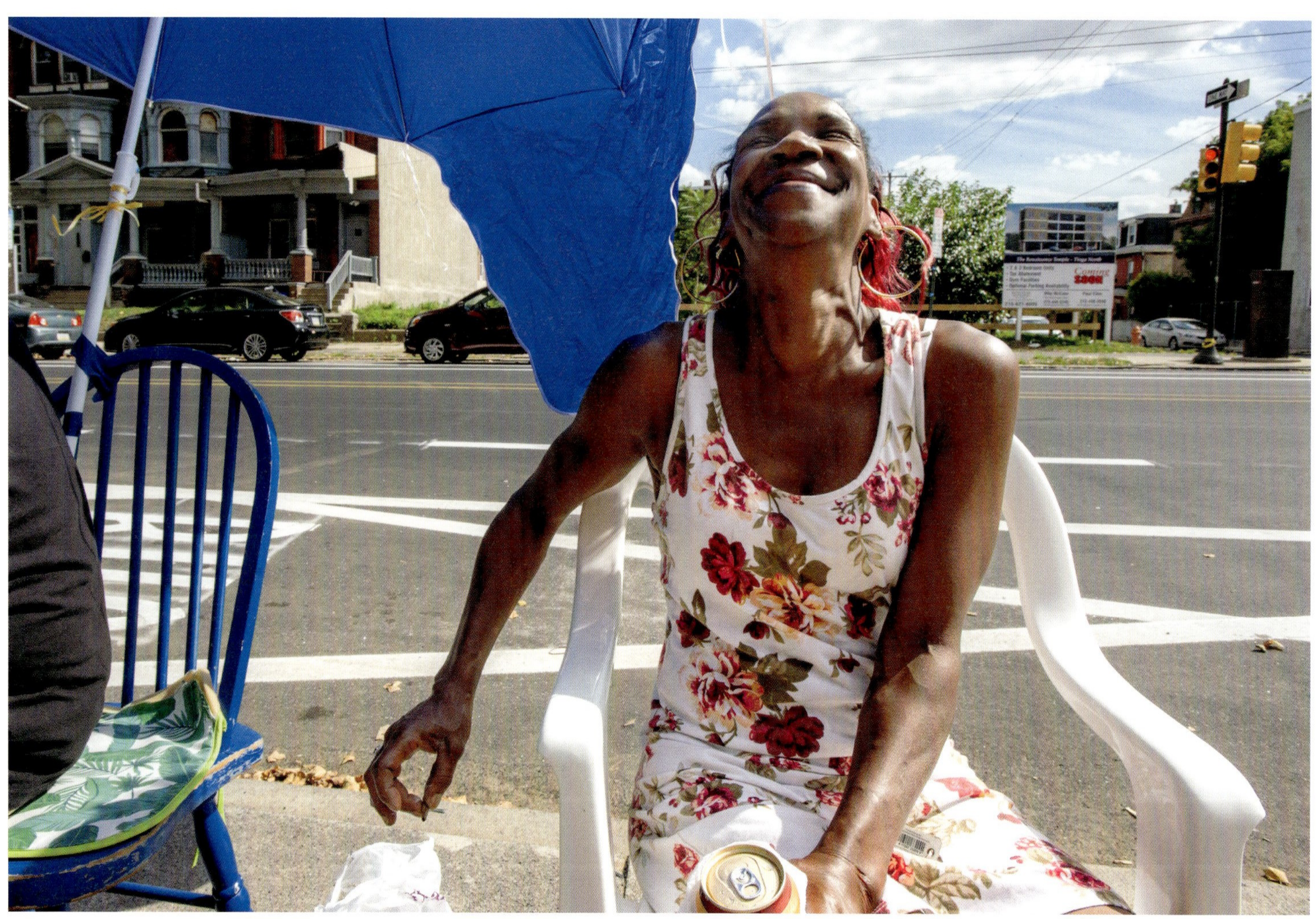

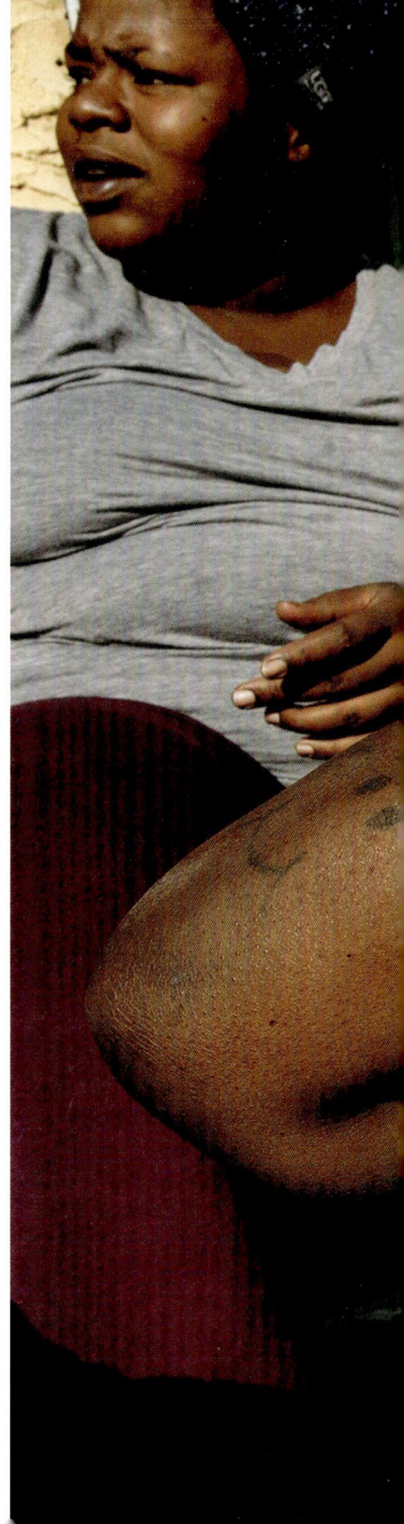

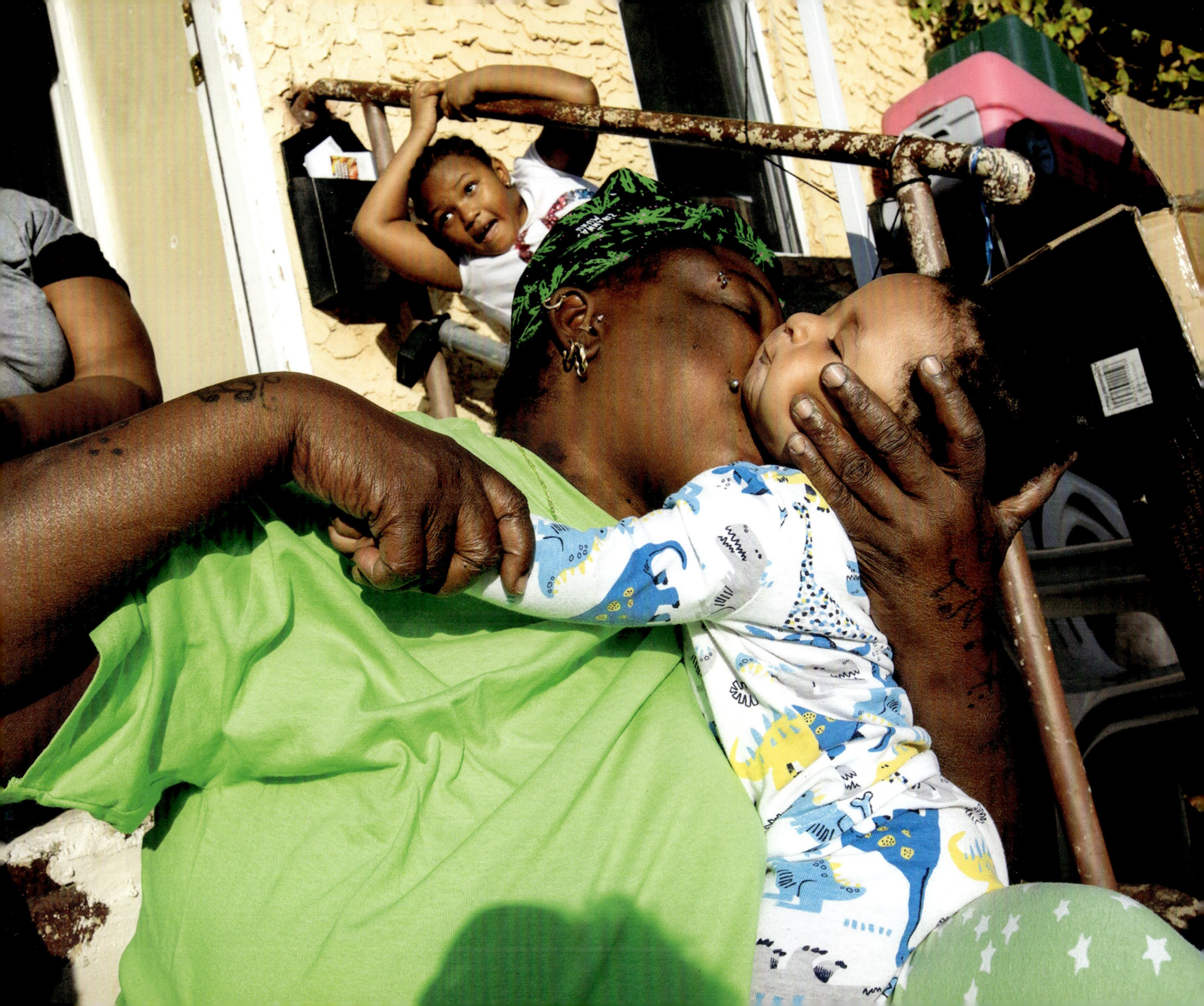

"What do you do with the demons in your head?"

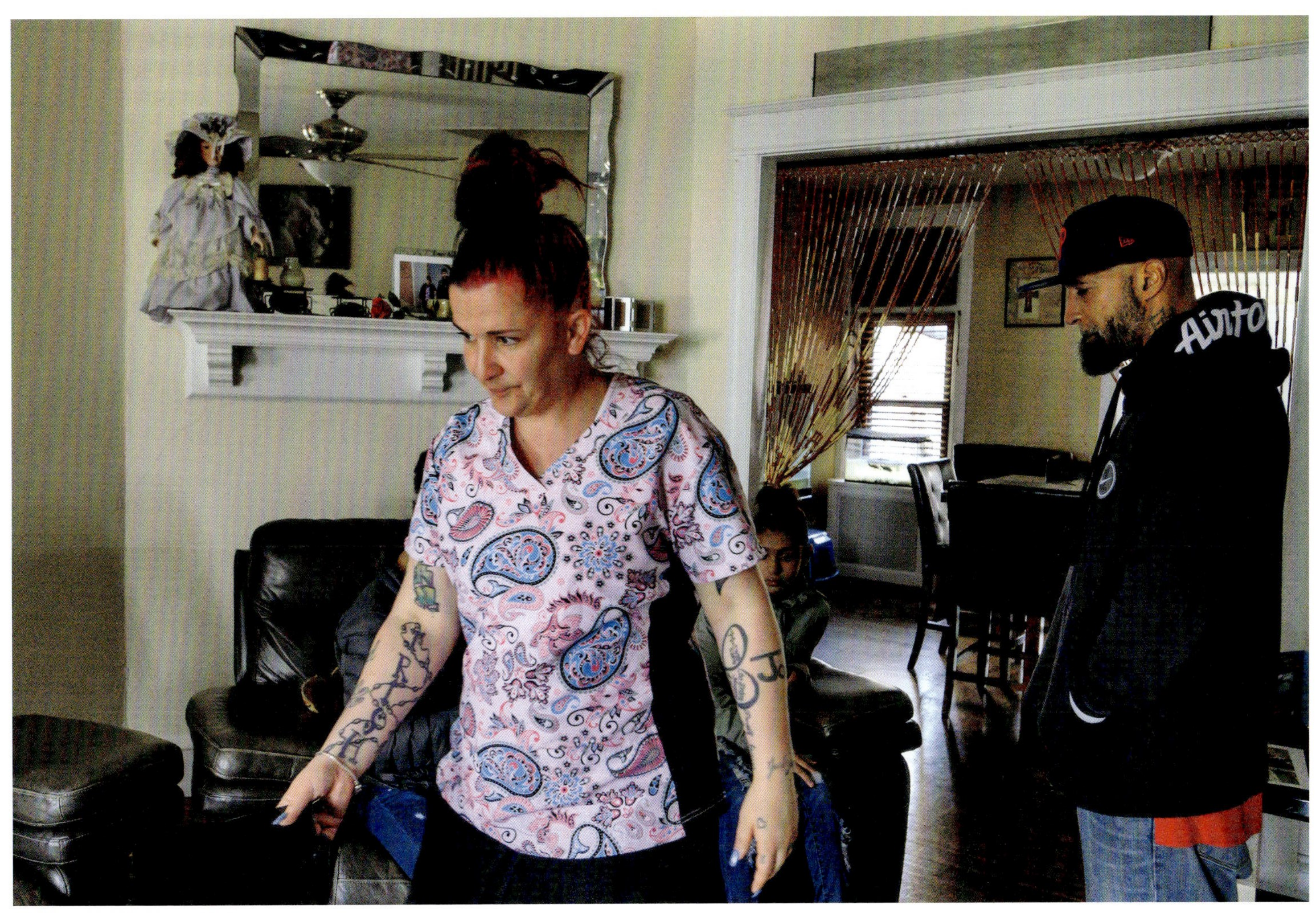

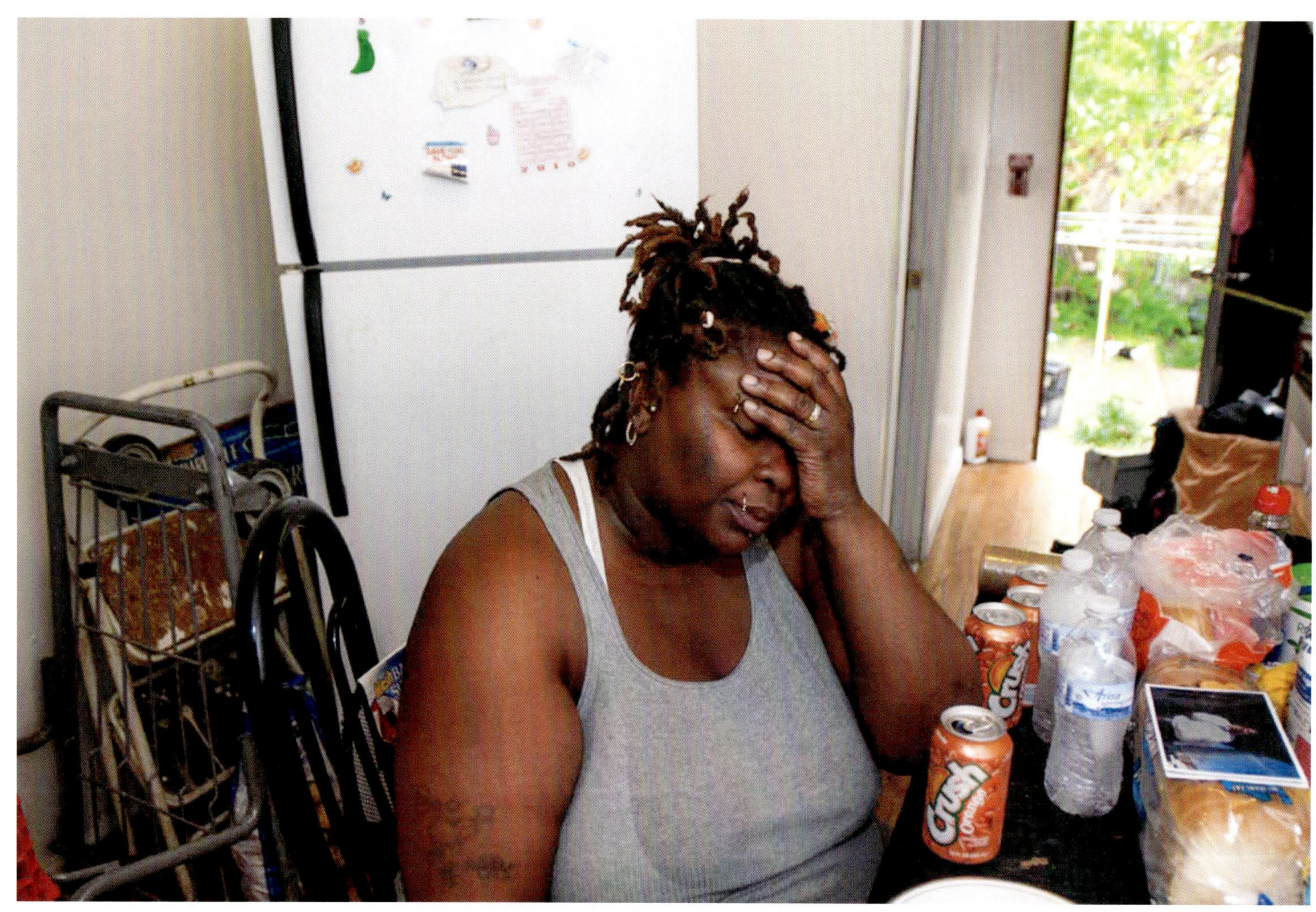

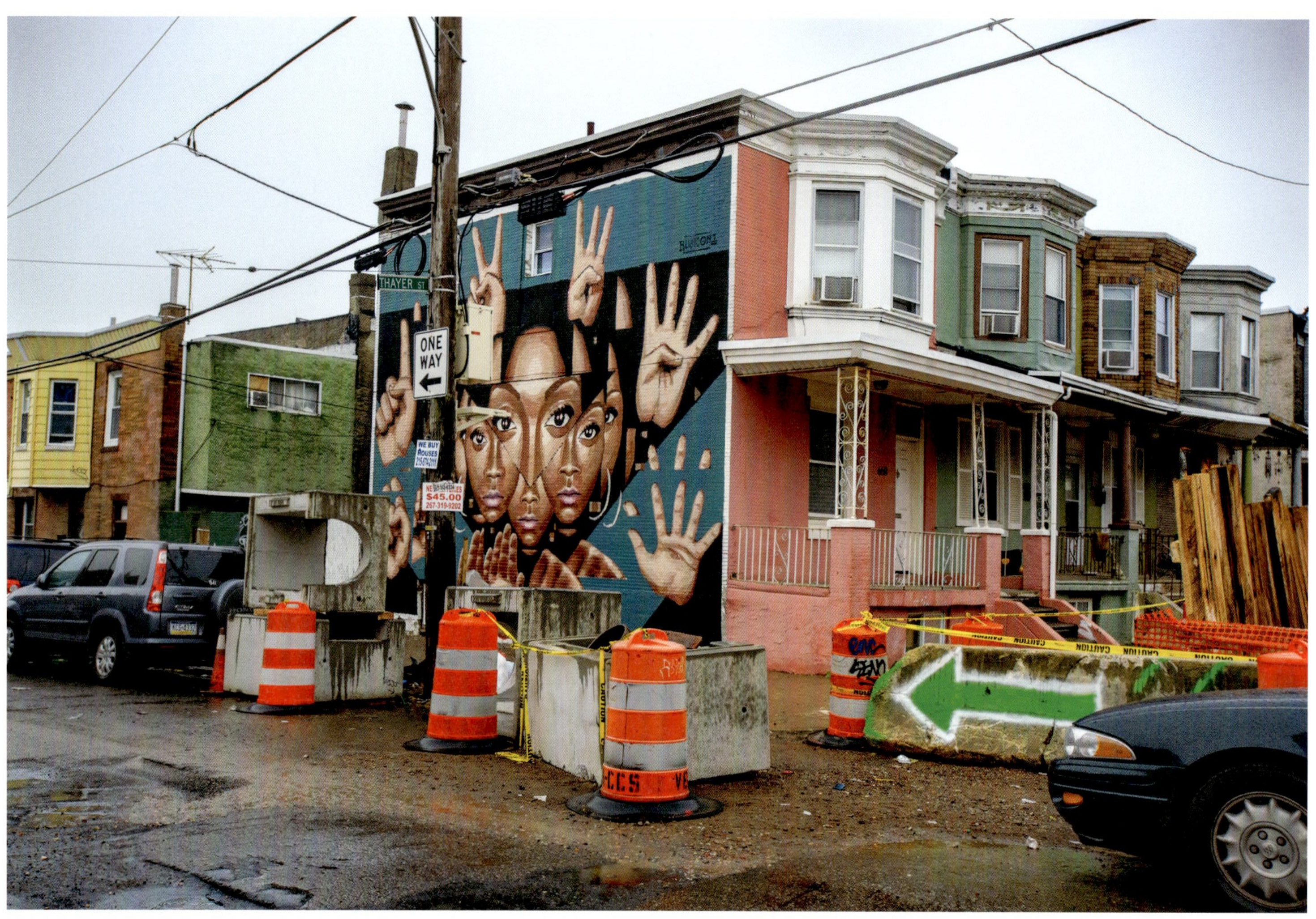

THAYER ST
ONE WAY
WE BUY
HOUSES
267-319-9202

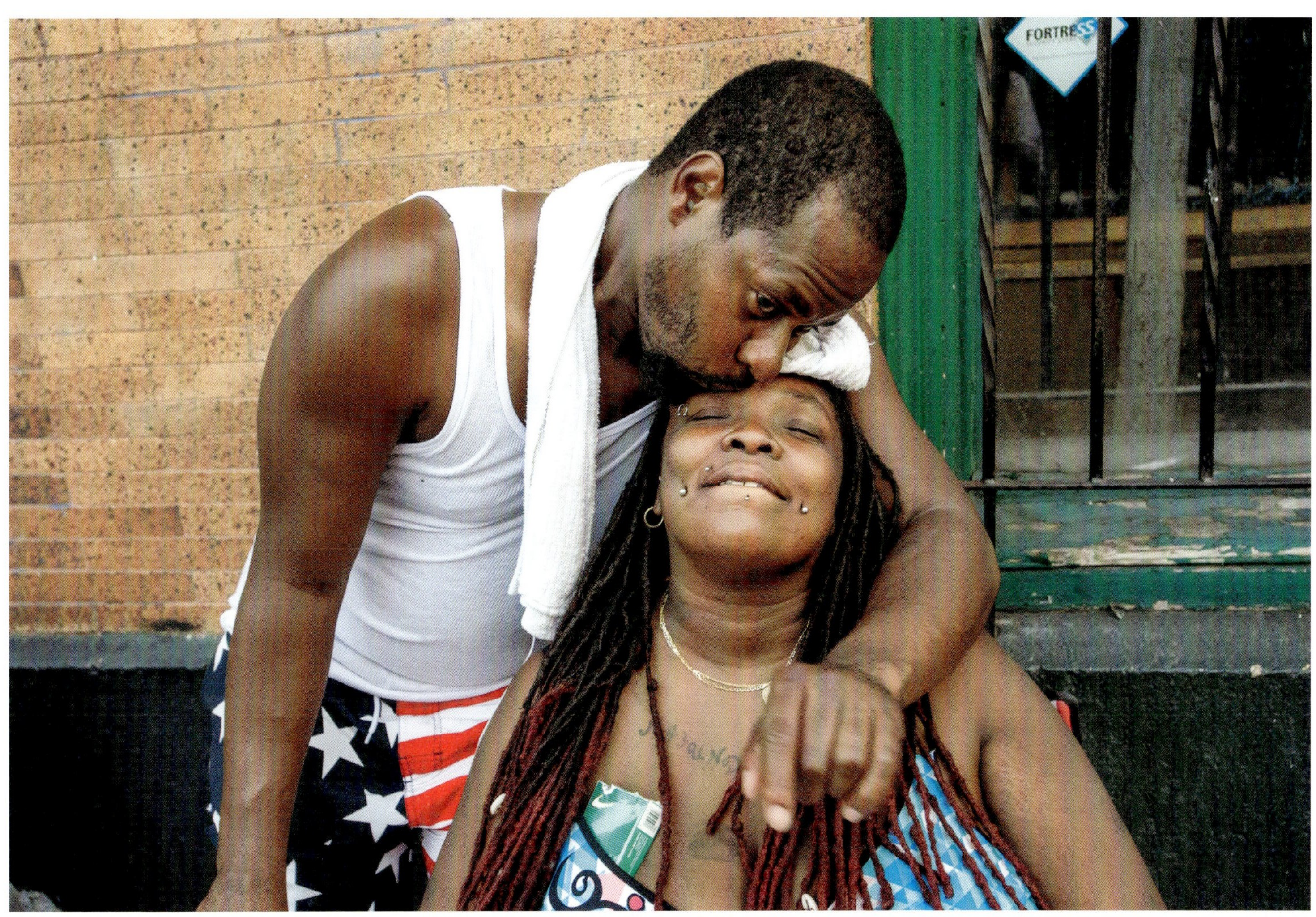
FORTRESS

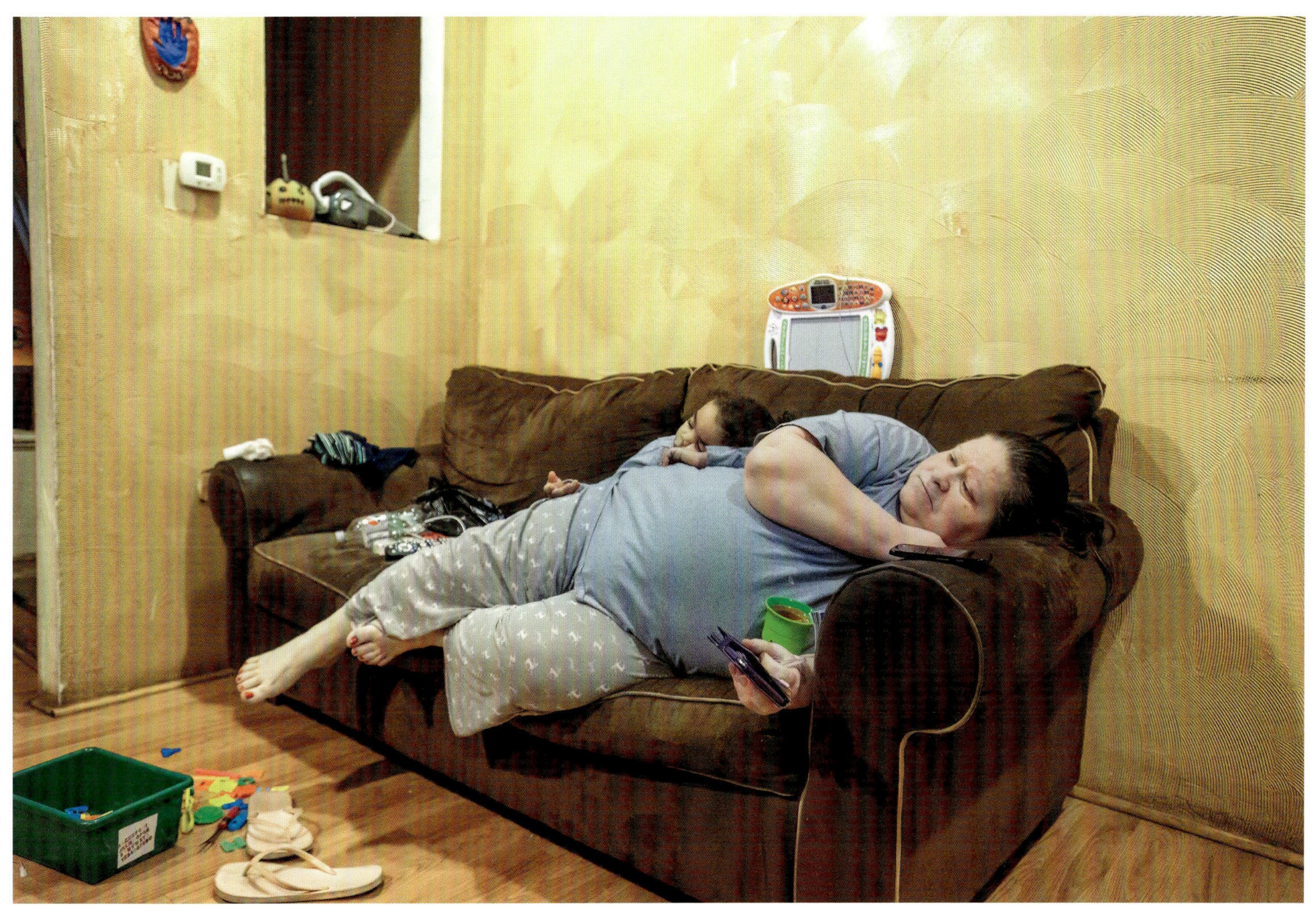

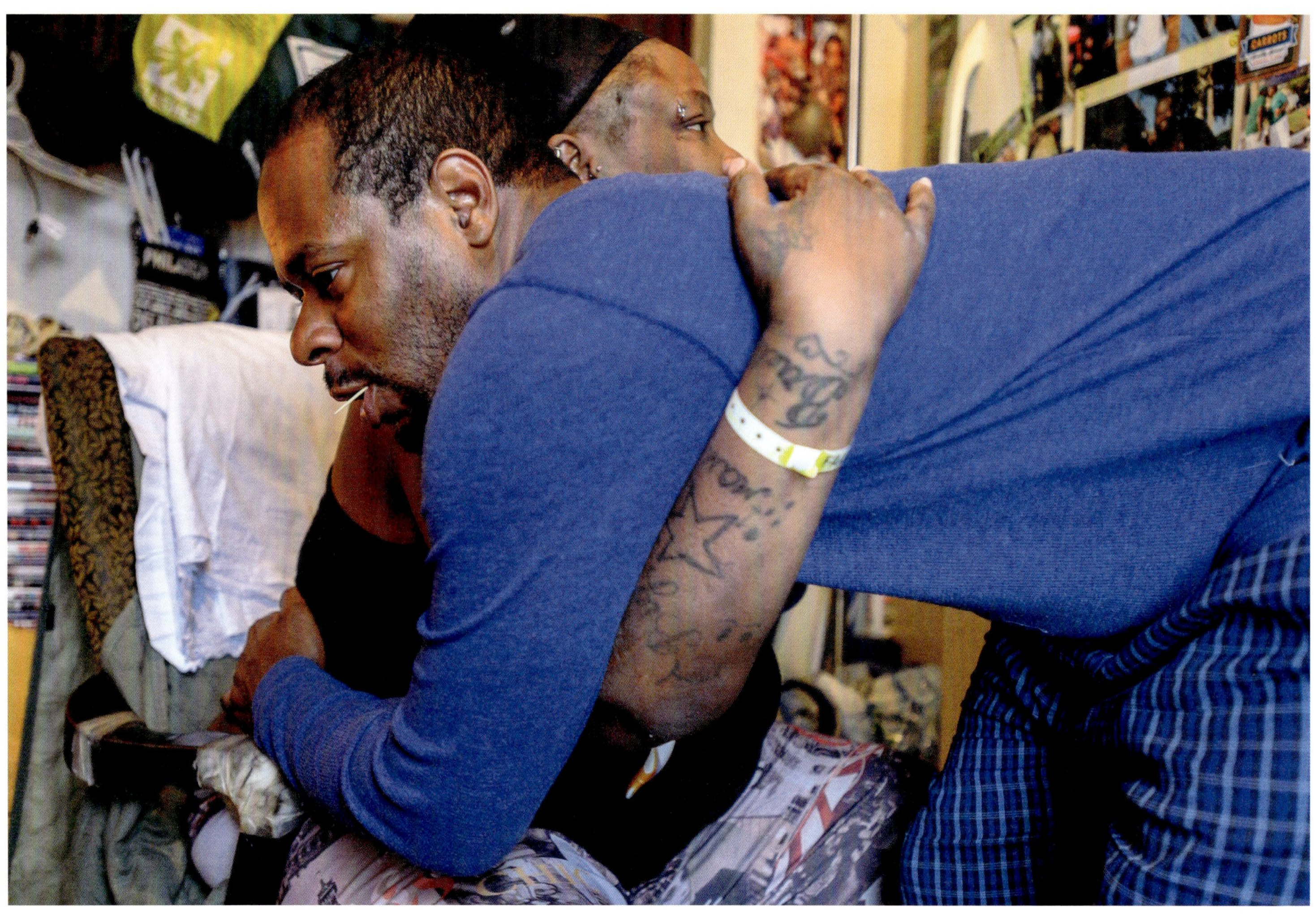

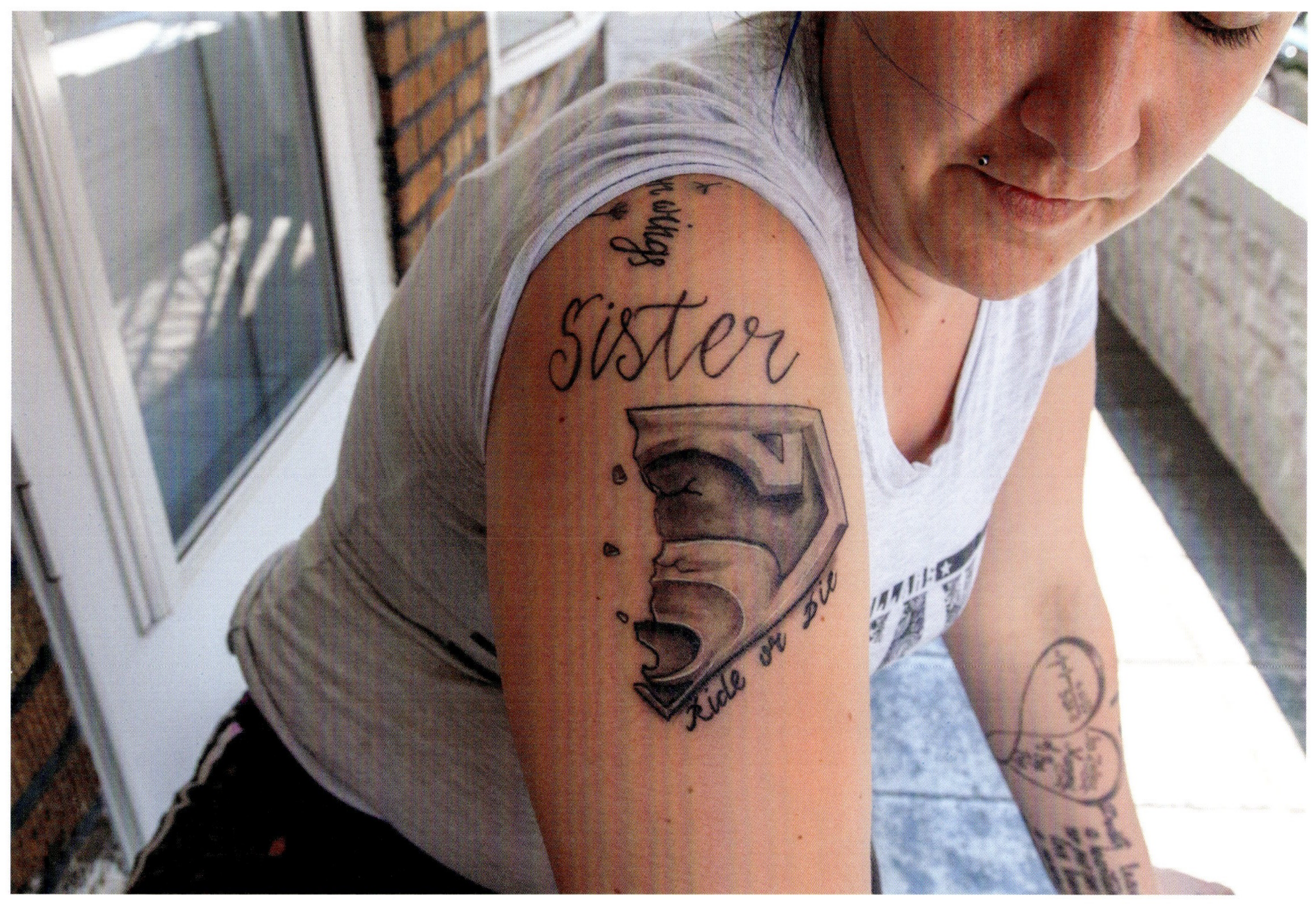

"I told Joe Bear he could stay with K and me to keep him safe and drug-free. While cleaning the bathroom, I found his works in the trash. He's been in jail in Maryland since then."

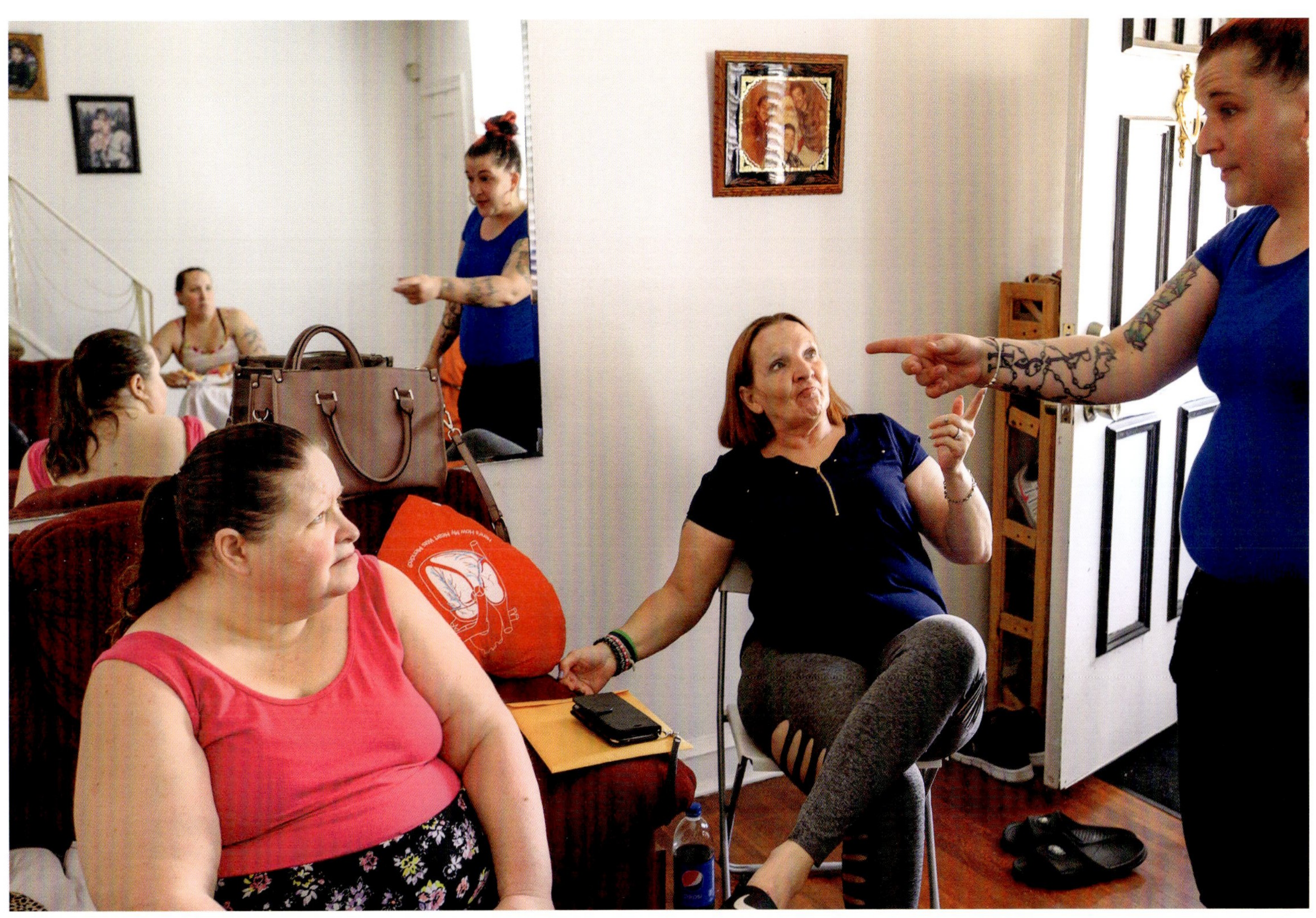

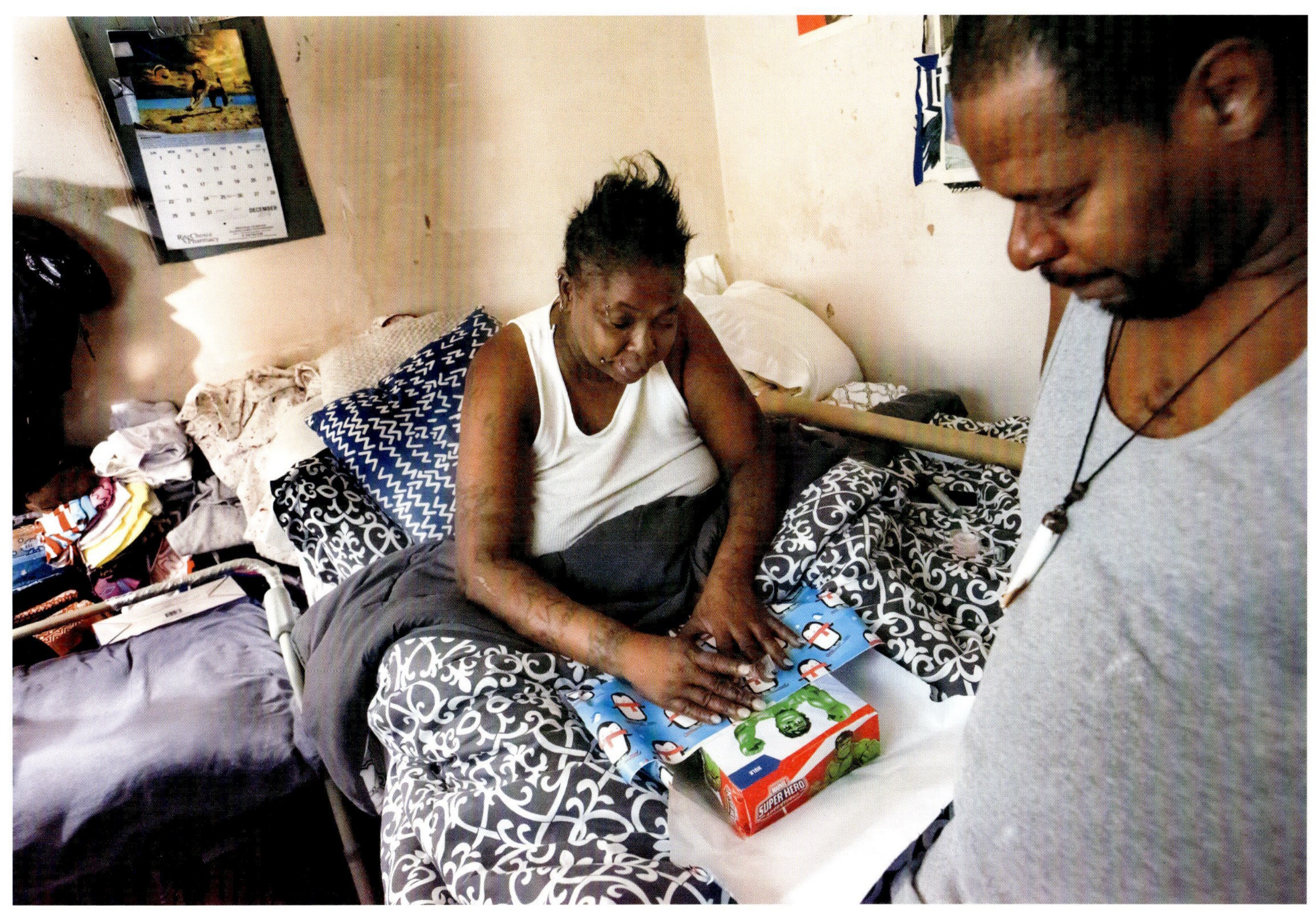

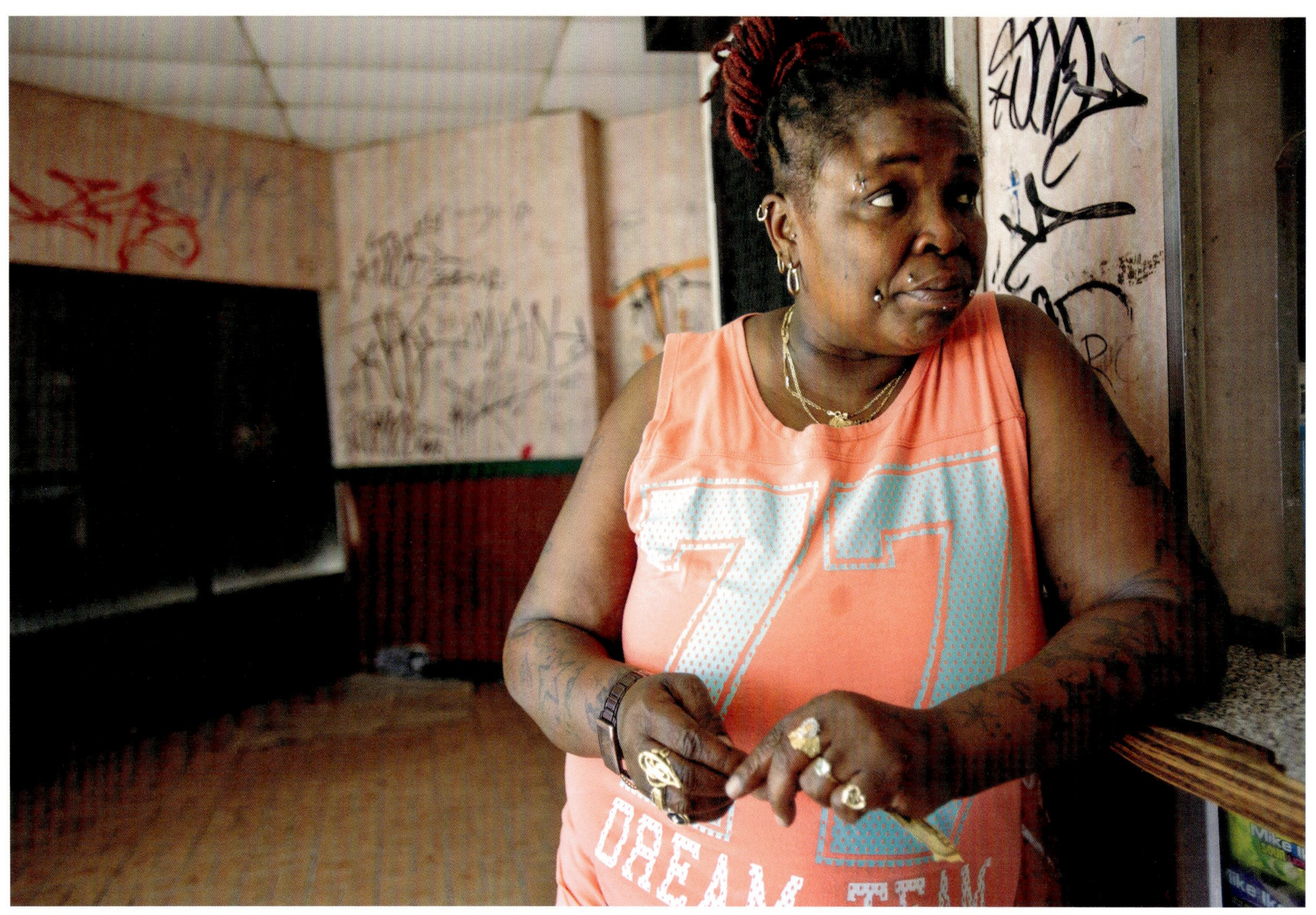

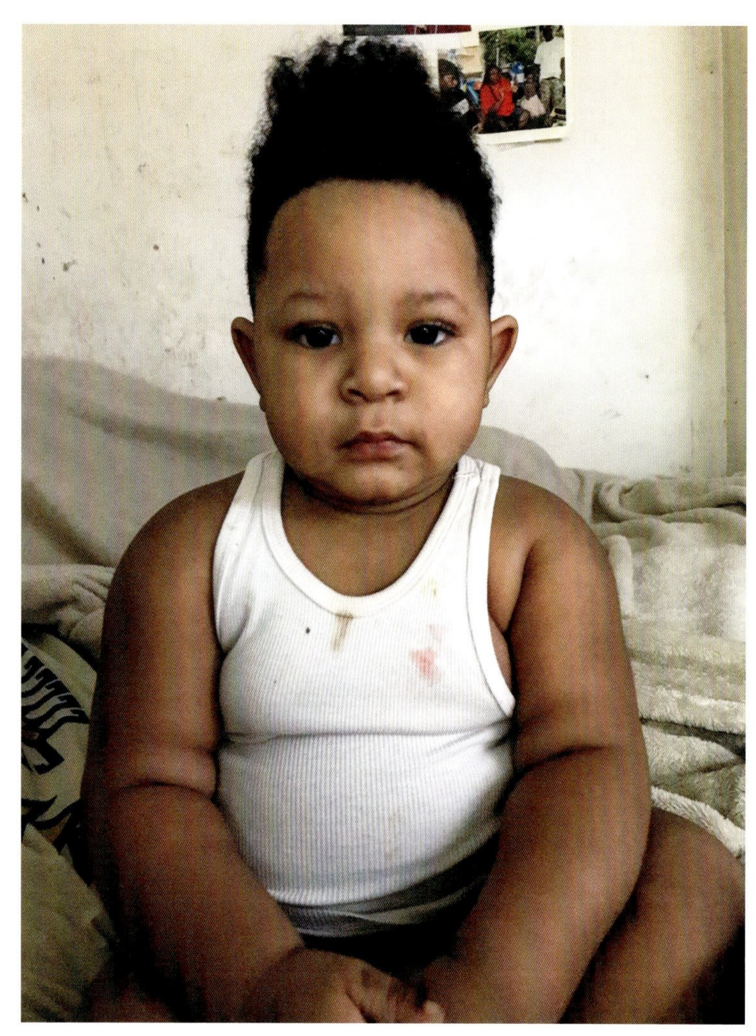

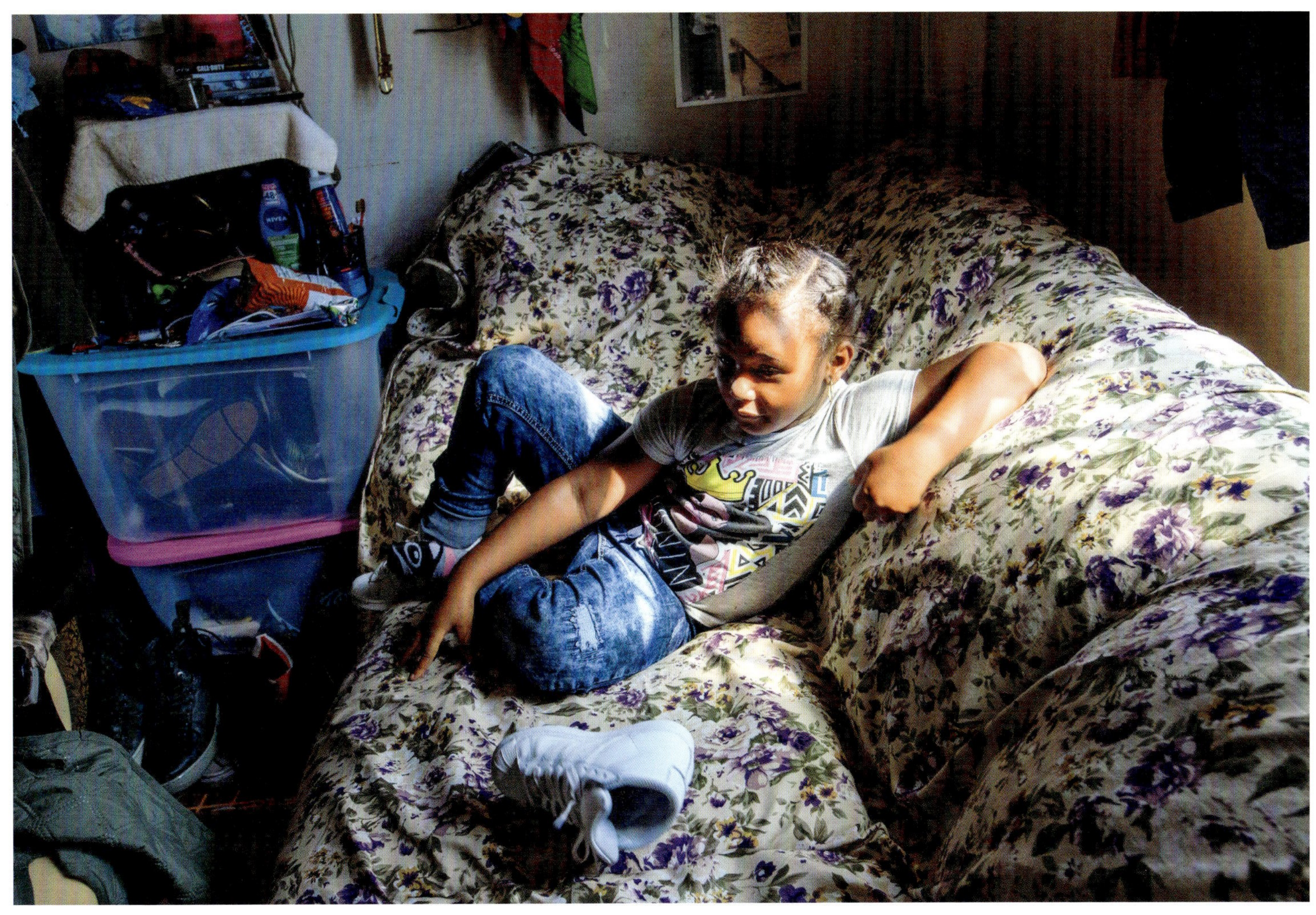

"I pushed Bella in the hall in front of me. We had to run inside, keeping low. The gunfire just went right in front of us."

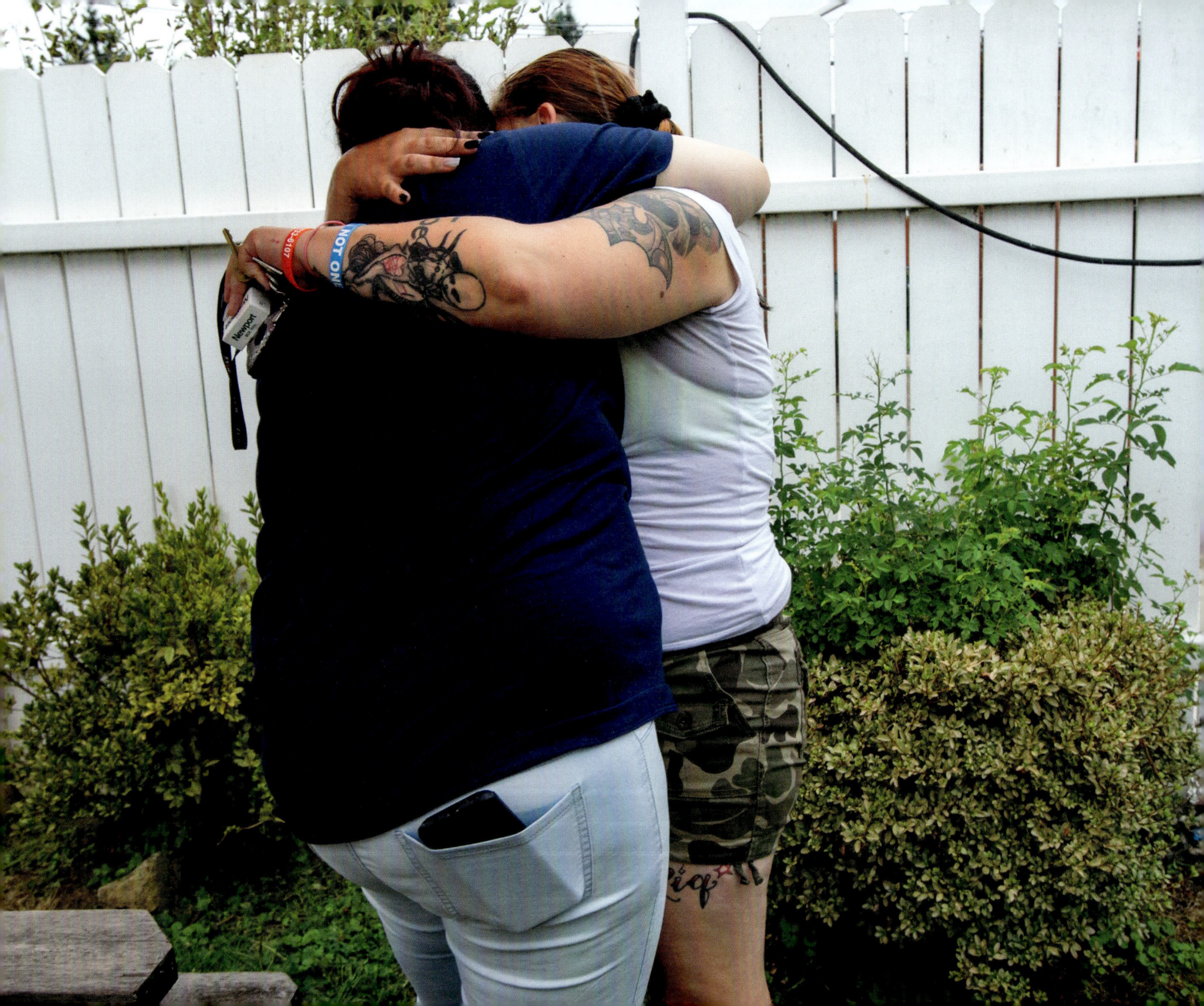

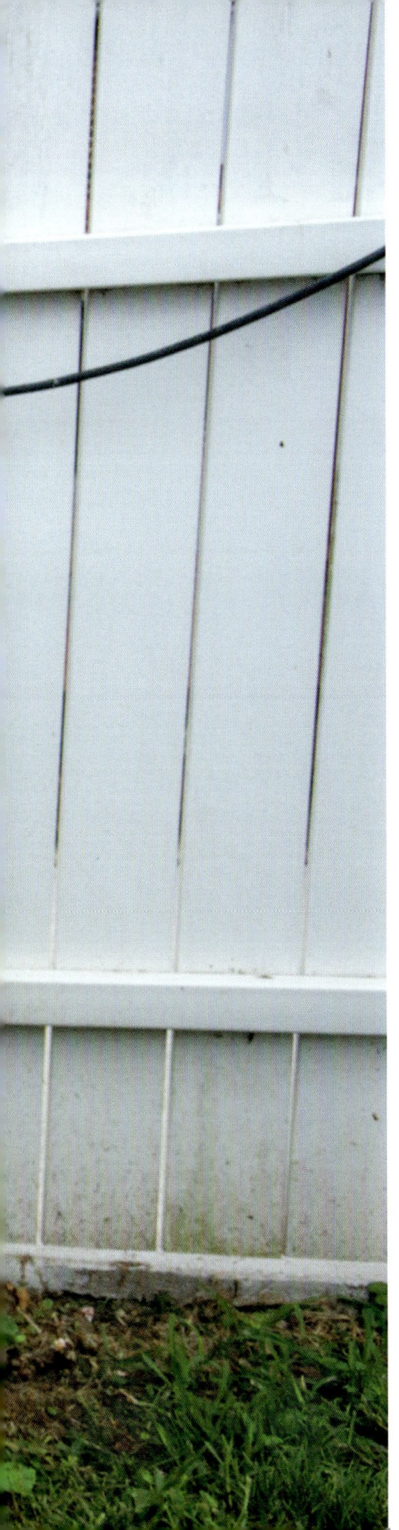

"You know she's got the camera. She's always got the camera."

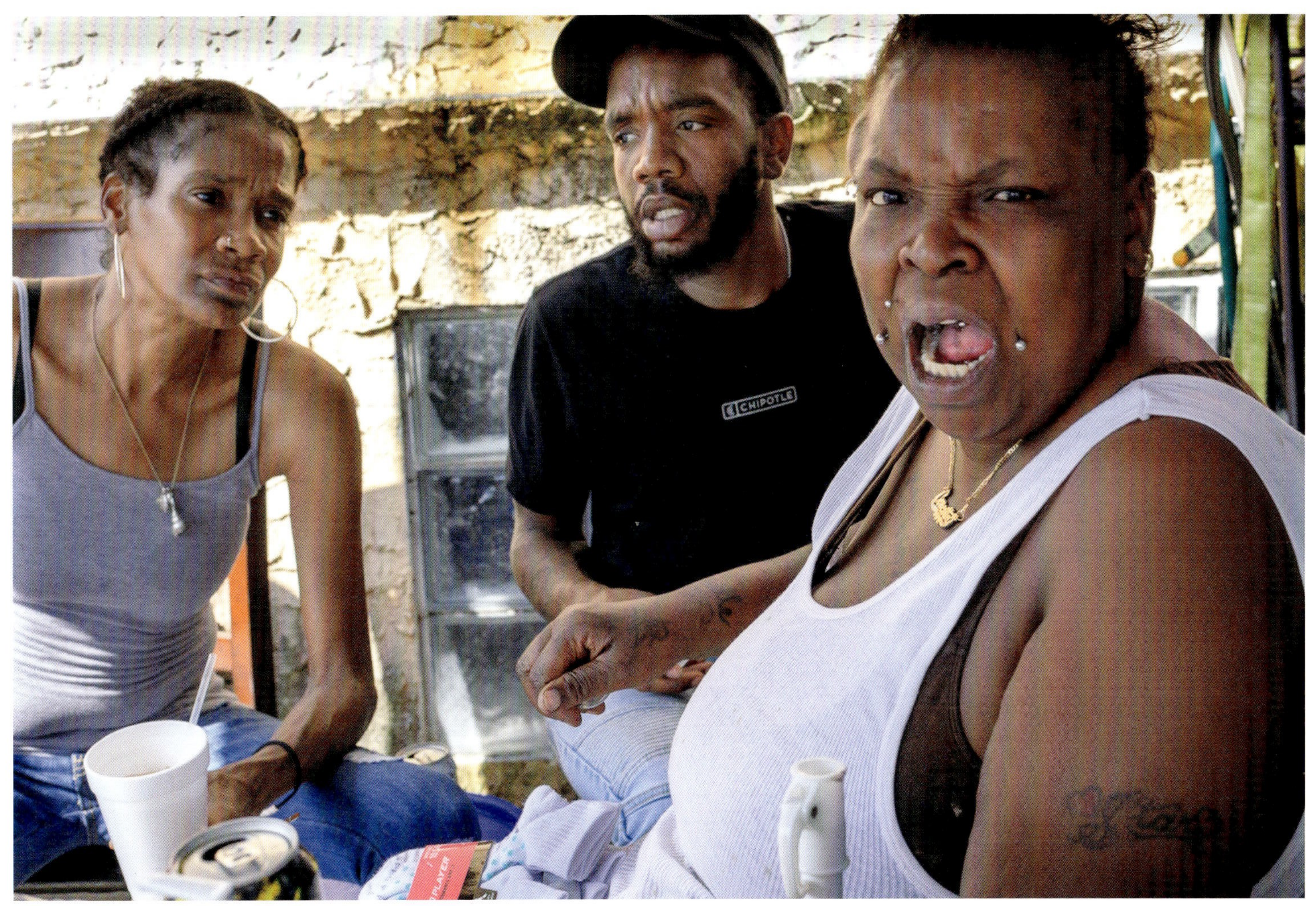

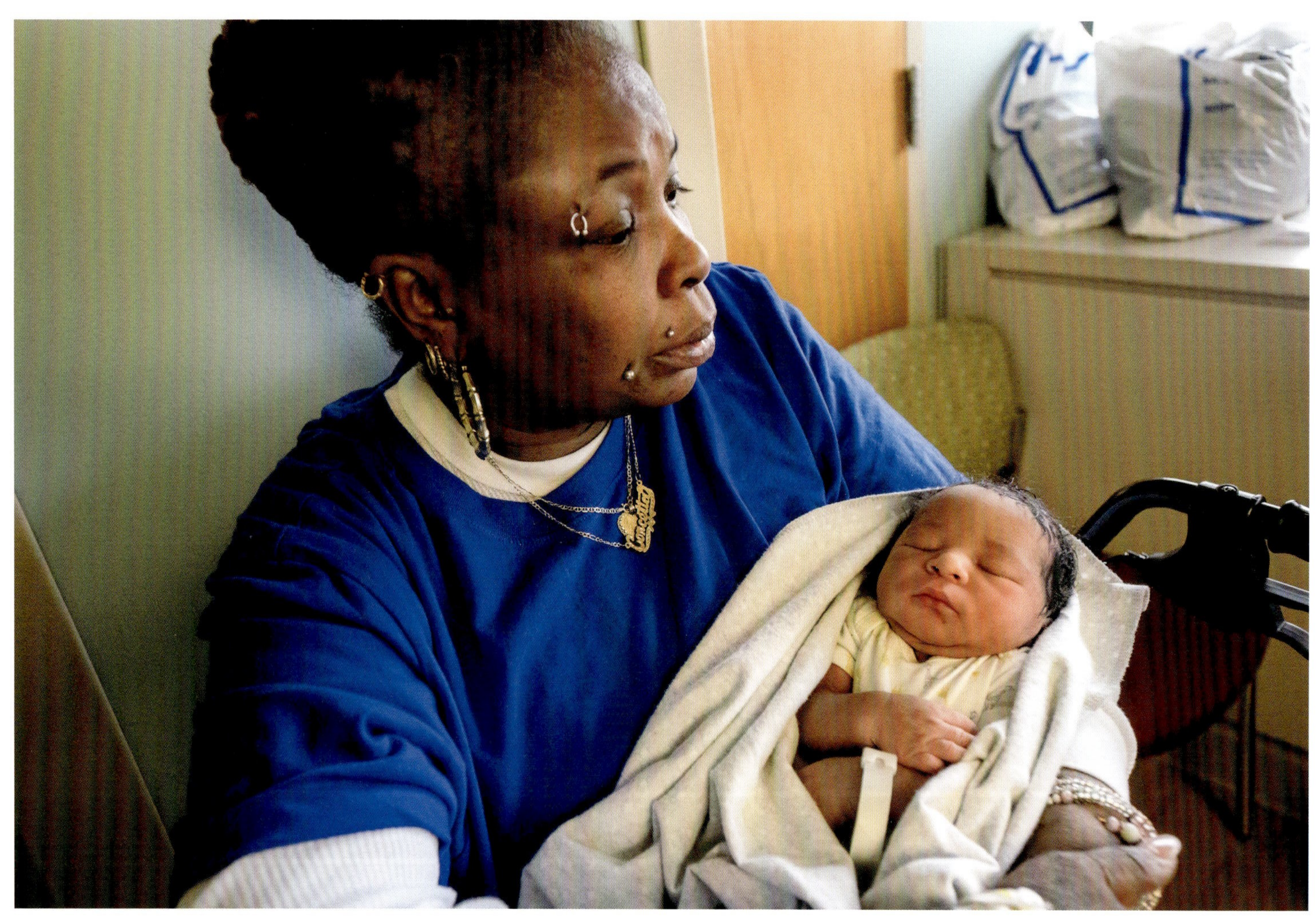

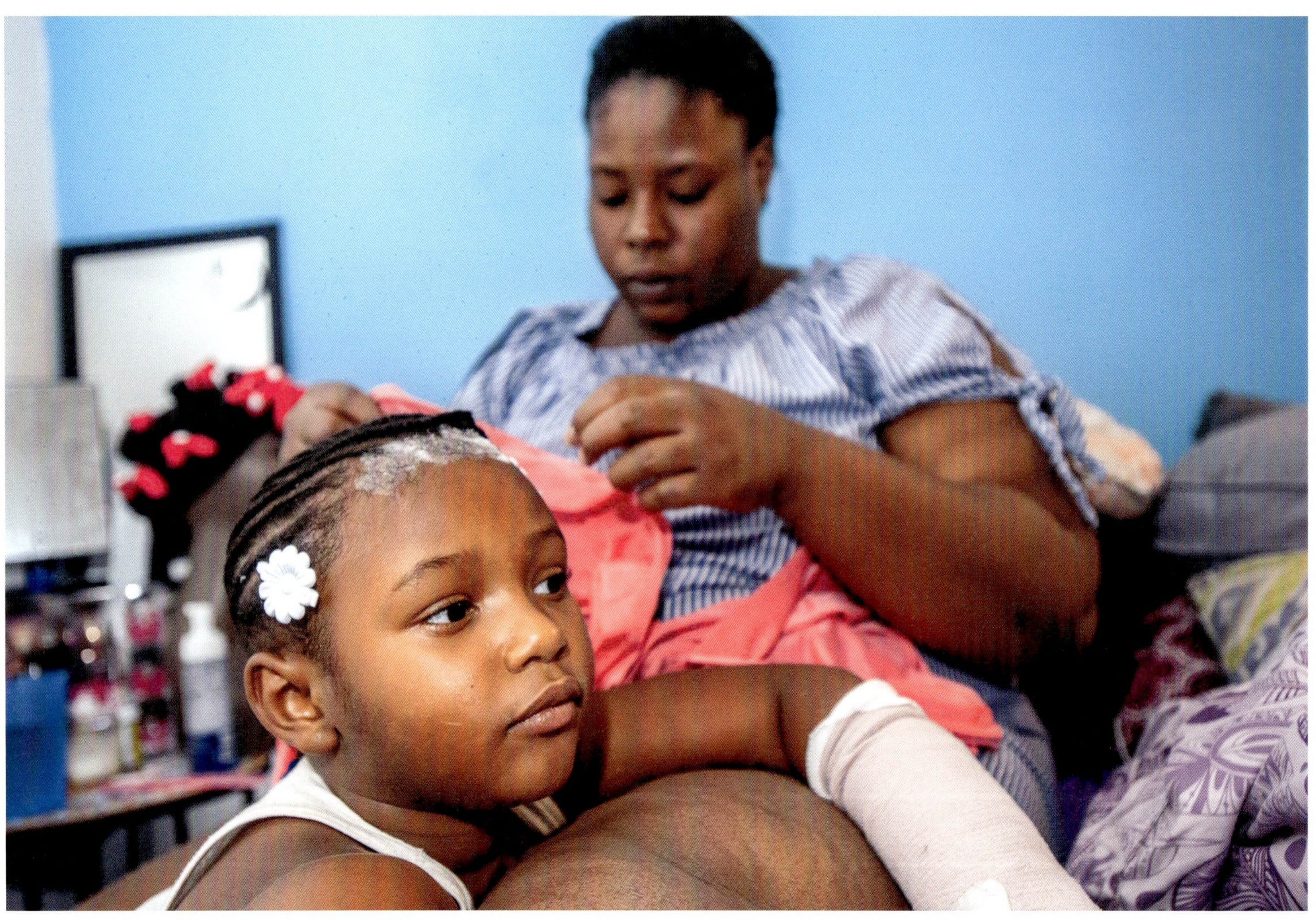

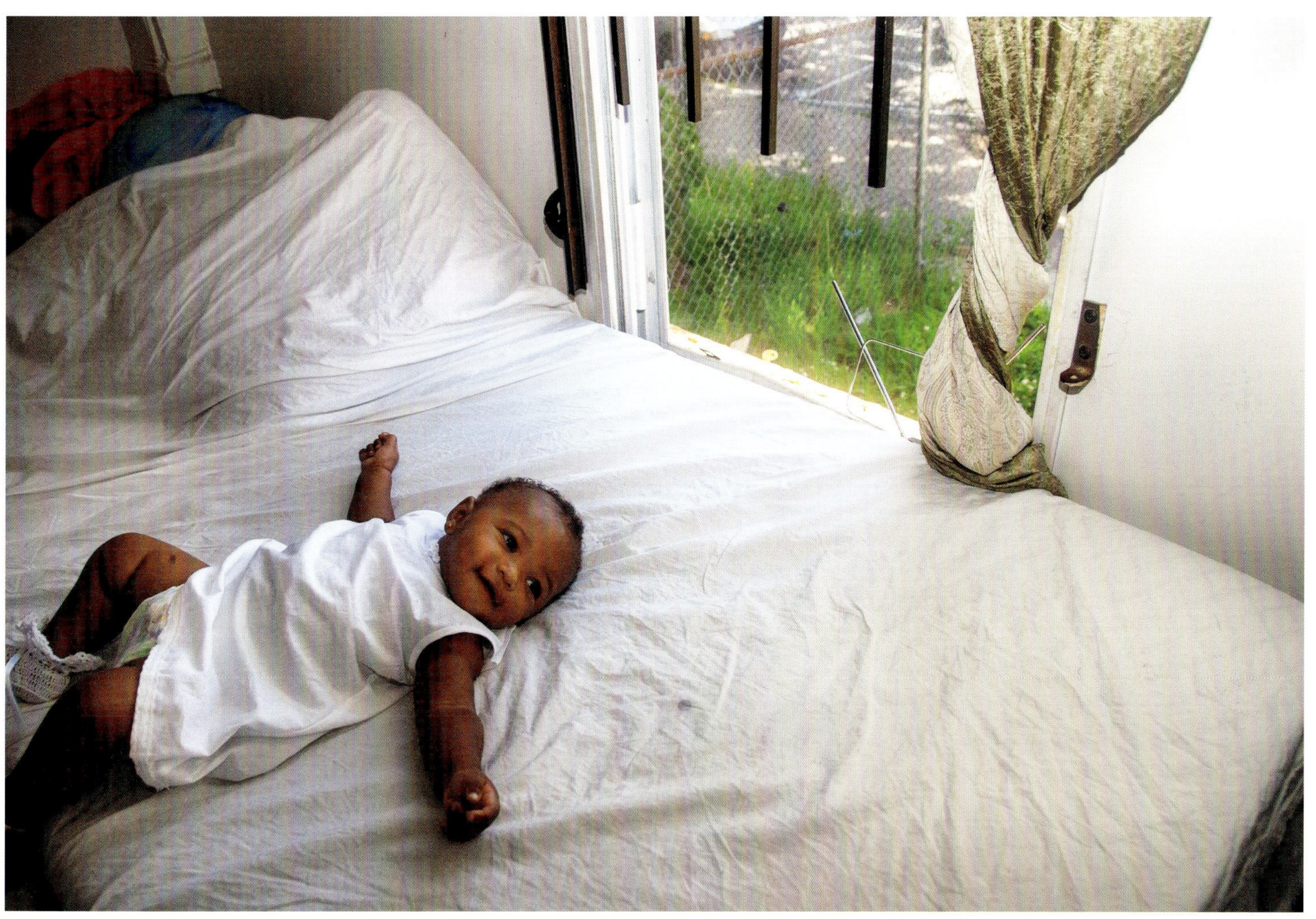

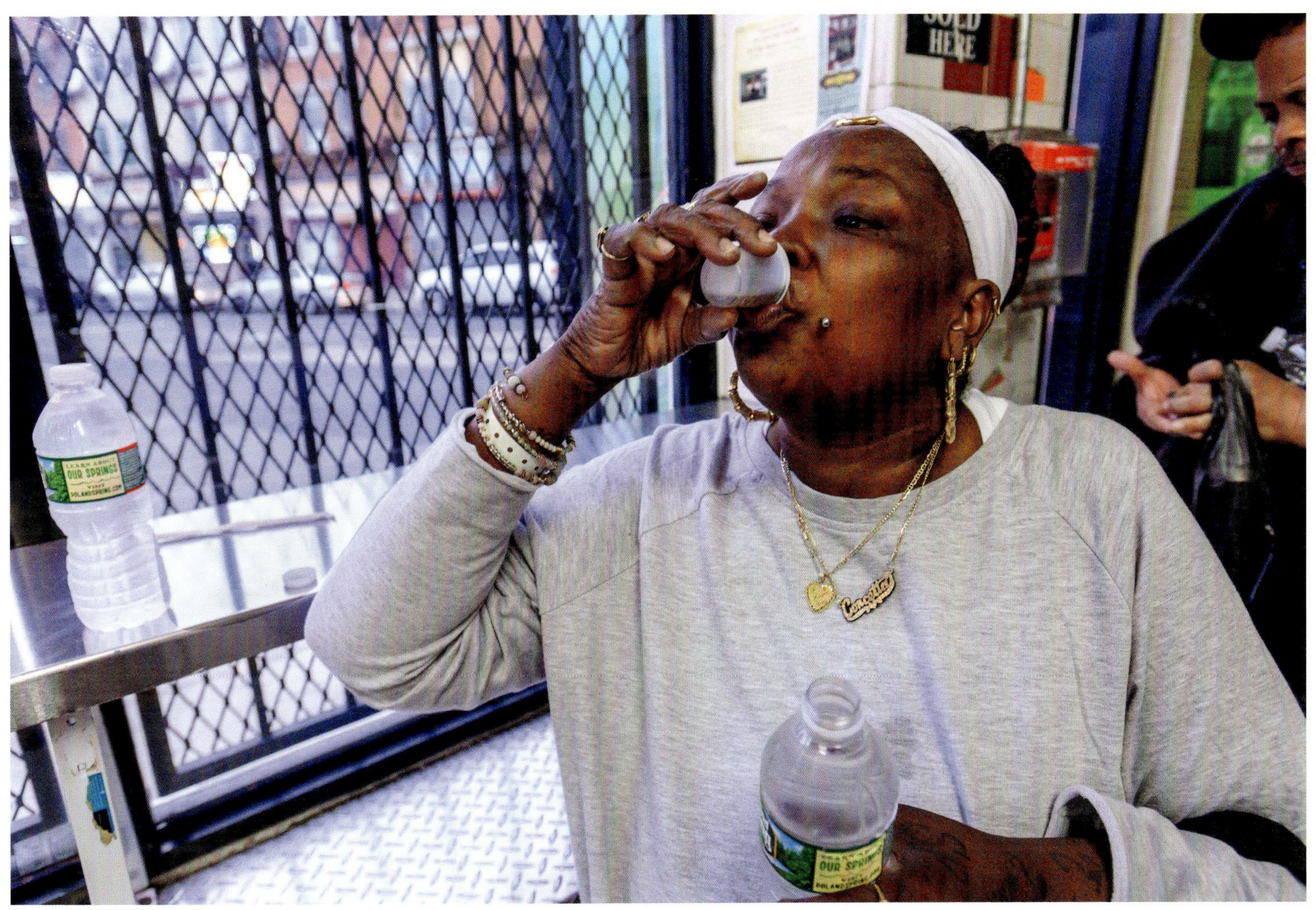

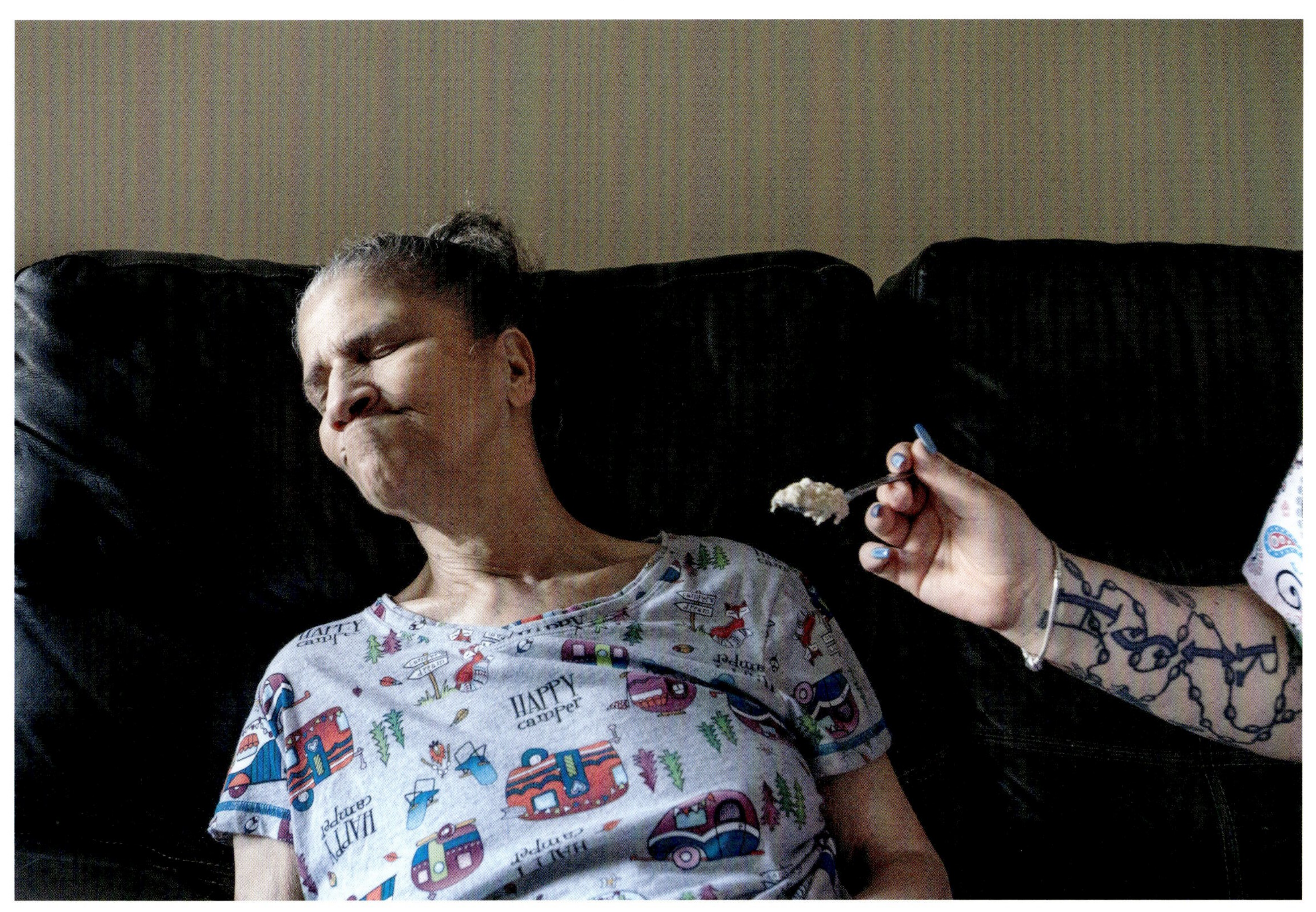
HAPPY
camper
HAPPY
camper

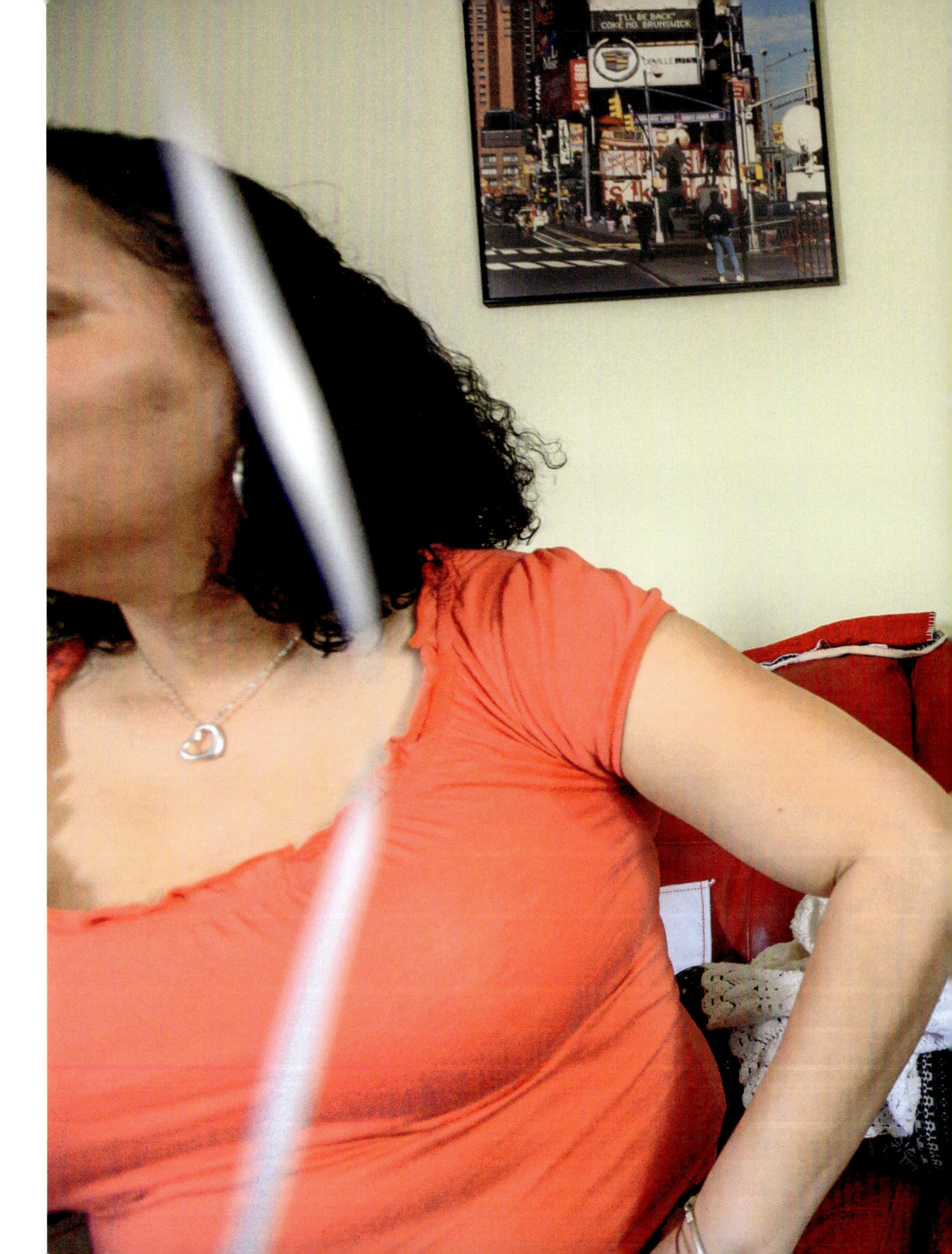

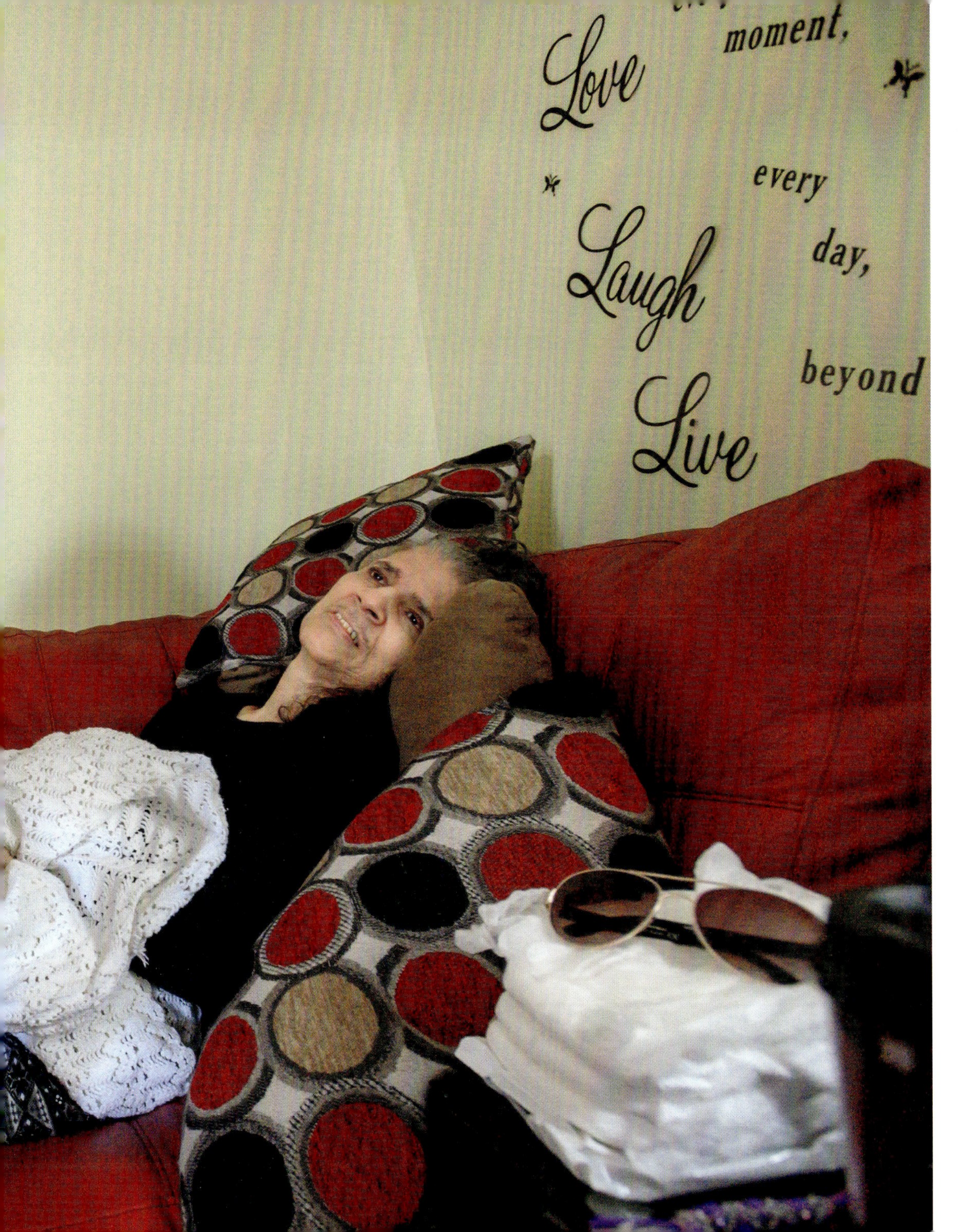
Love moment,
every
Laugh day,
Live beyond

"My nephew just passed away from Covid. He was only 23 but he had lots of health problems. And then this girl I knew from rehab just overdosed. I got two funerals this week."

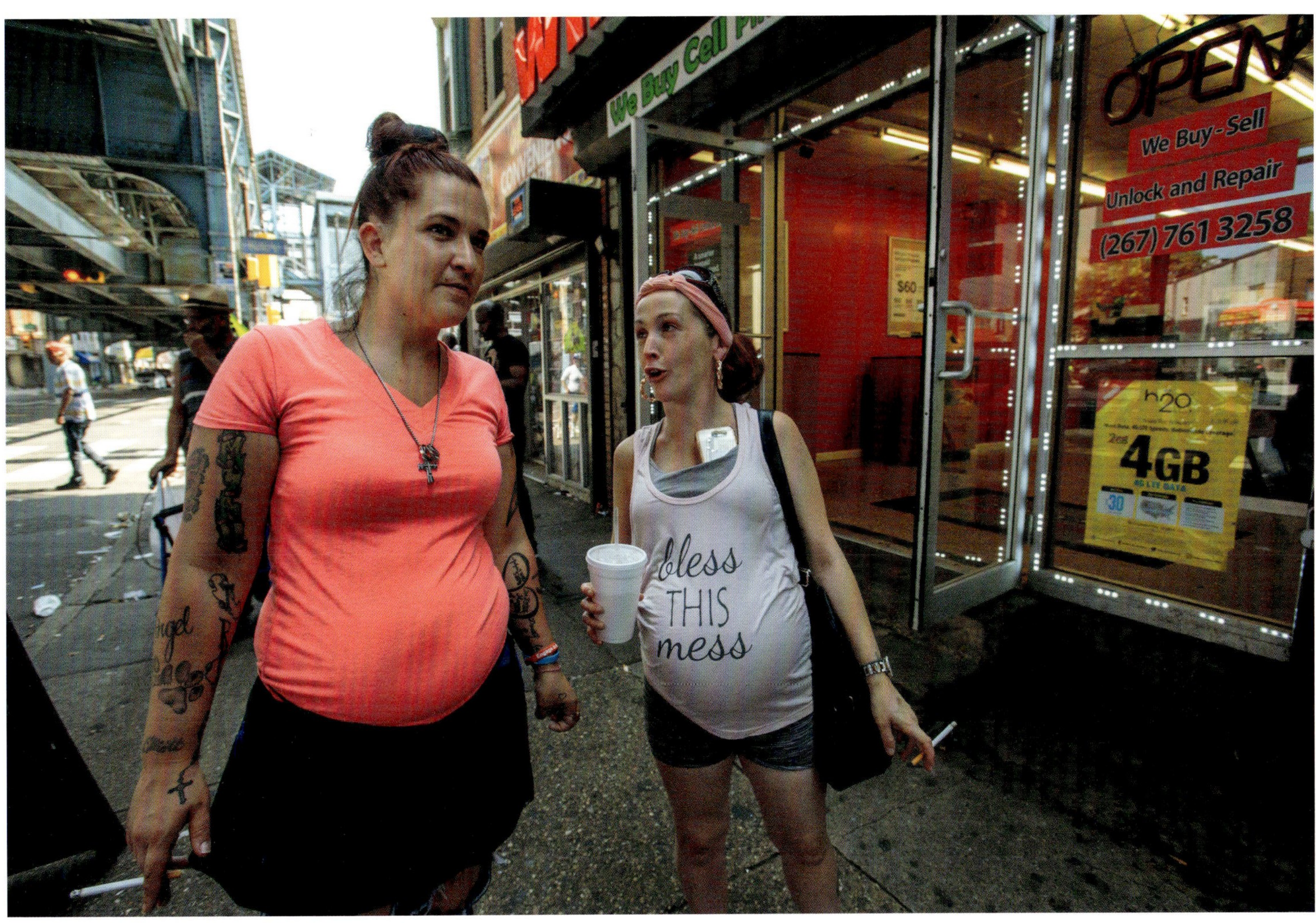
We Buy Cell Phones
OPEN
We Buy - Sell
Unlock and Repair
(267) 761 3258
$60
h2o
4GB
bless
THIS
mess

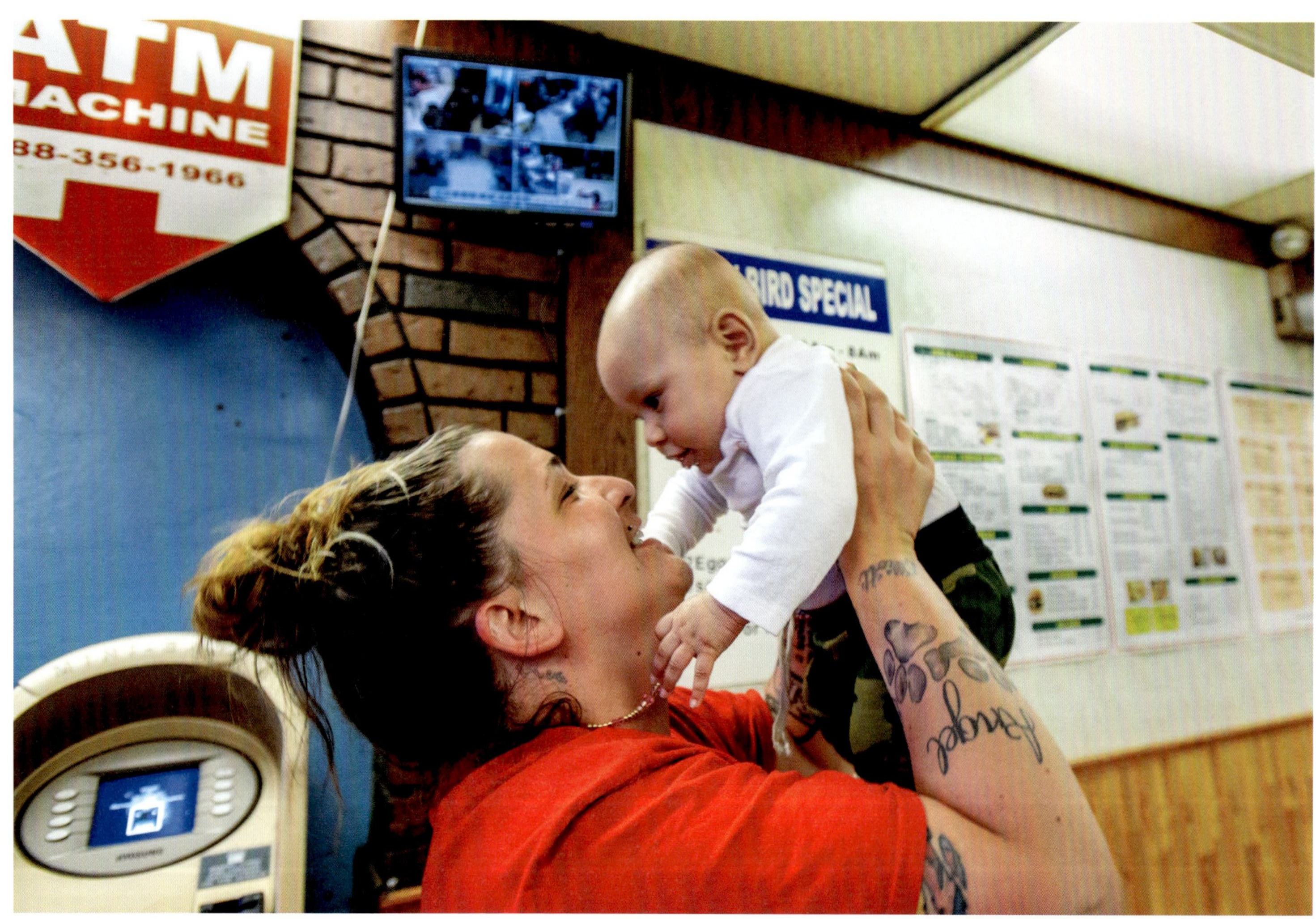

"Kat checked on him before she left for work. When Mom-Mom went to get him around nine, he wasn't breathing. The cops were all over the place.

As they should be."

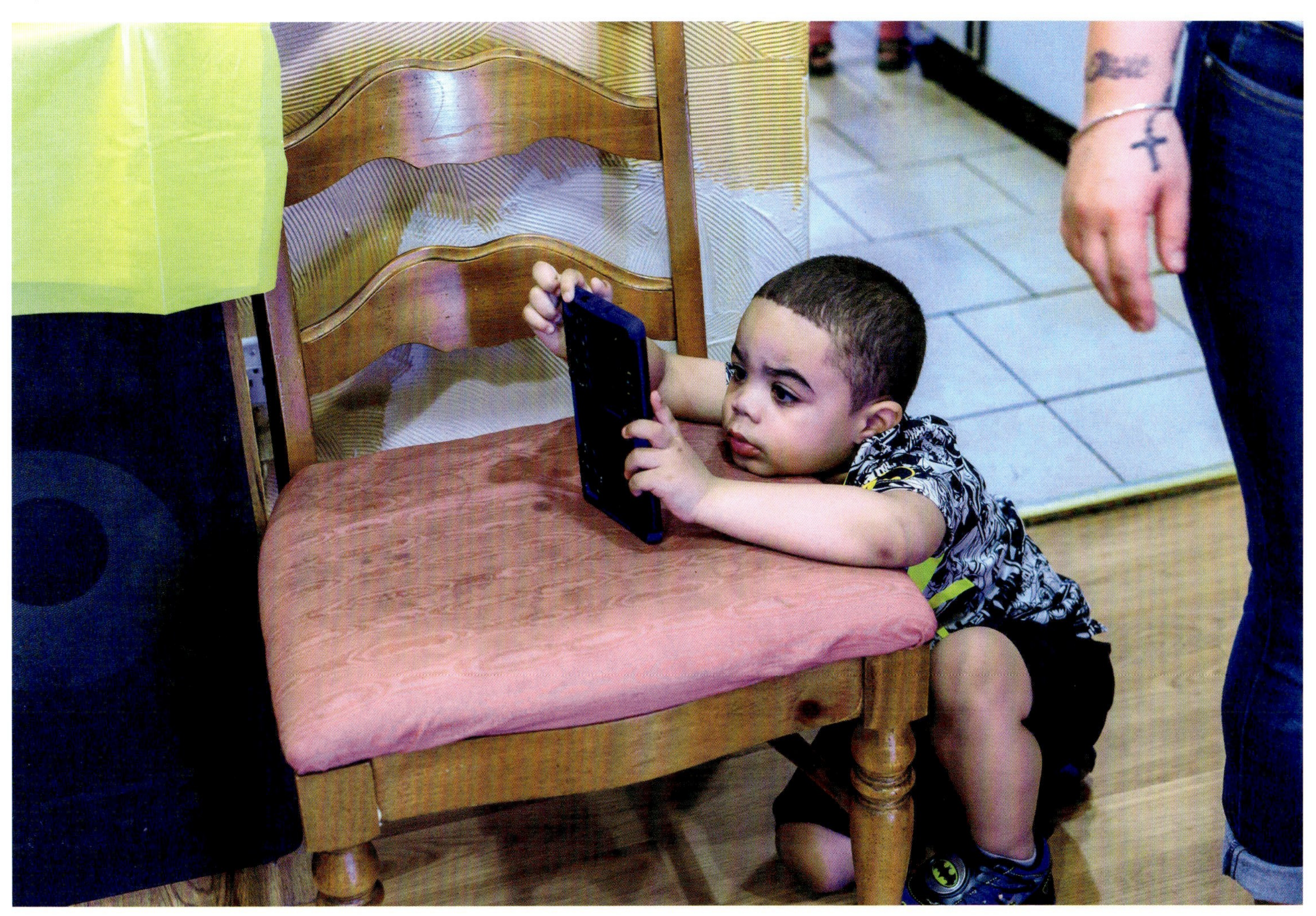

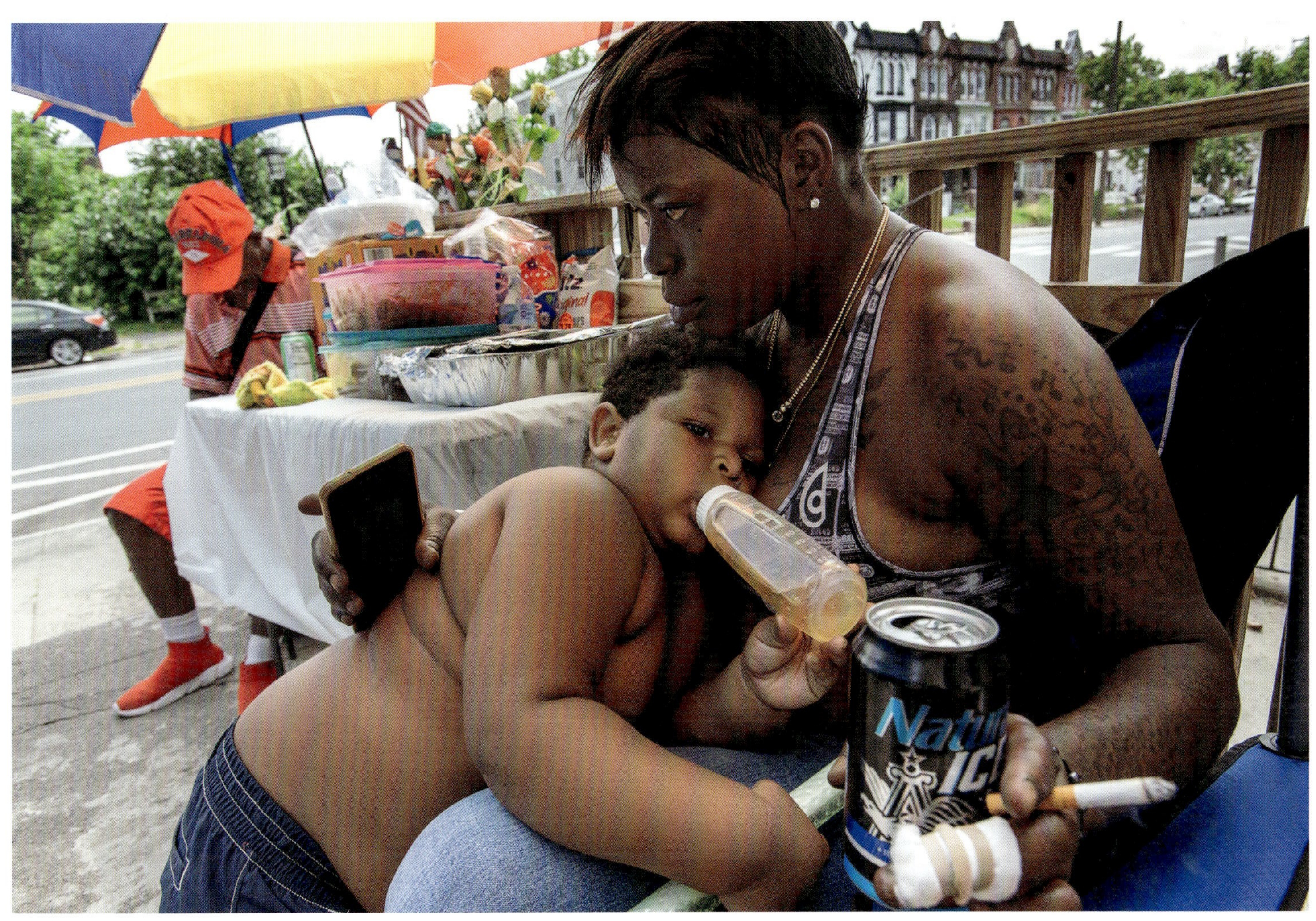

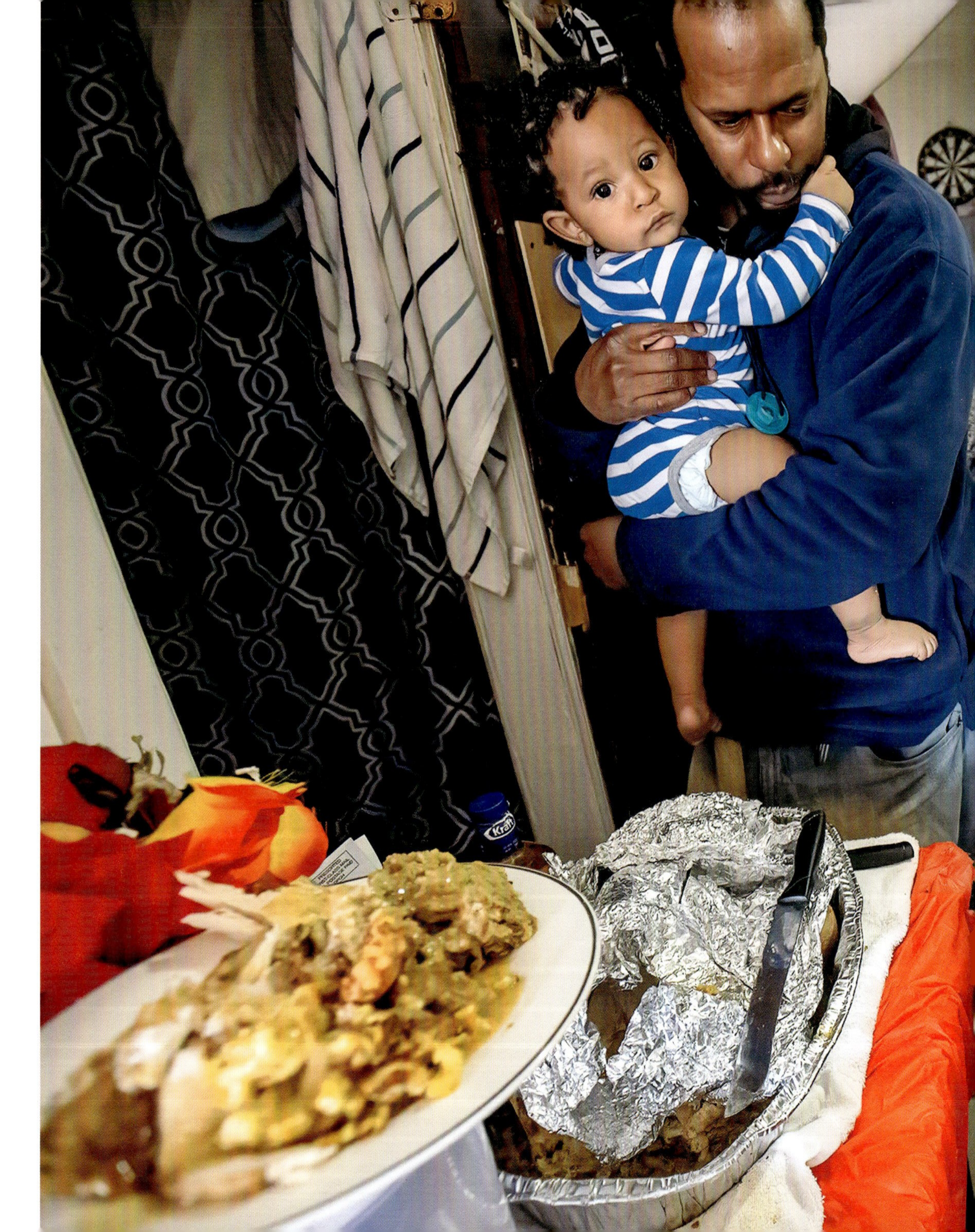

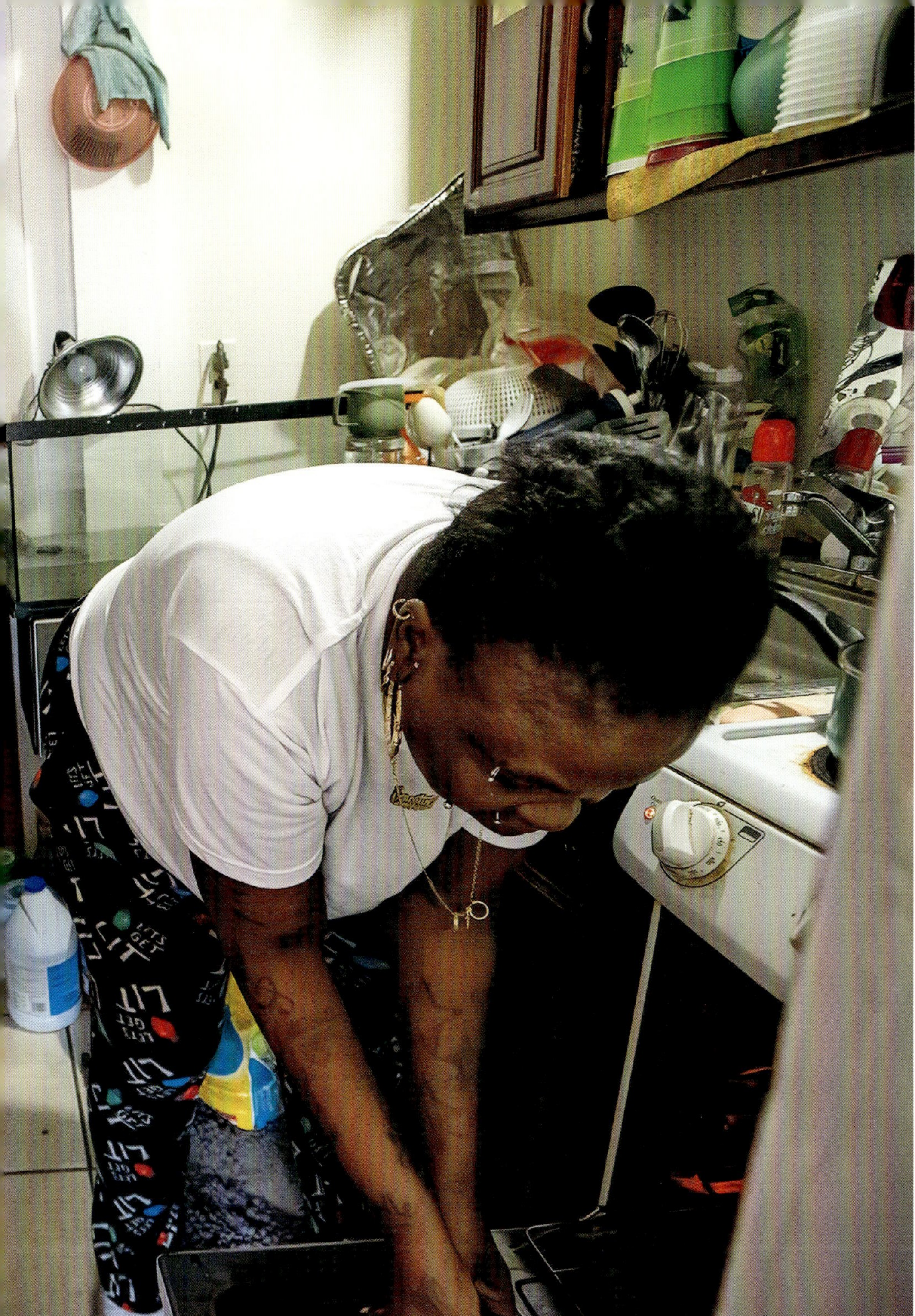

"He better not have Covid. They say Bryce might have the Covid. I will kill myself if anything happens to my grandson. Oh, God. Oh, God. I want to die."

"Mom. Please."

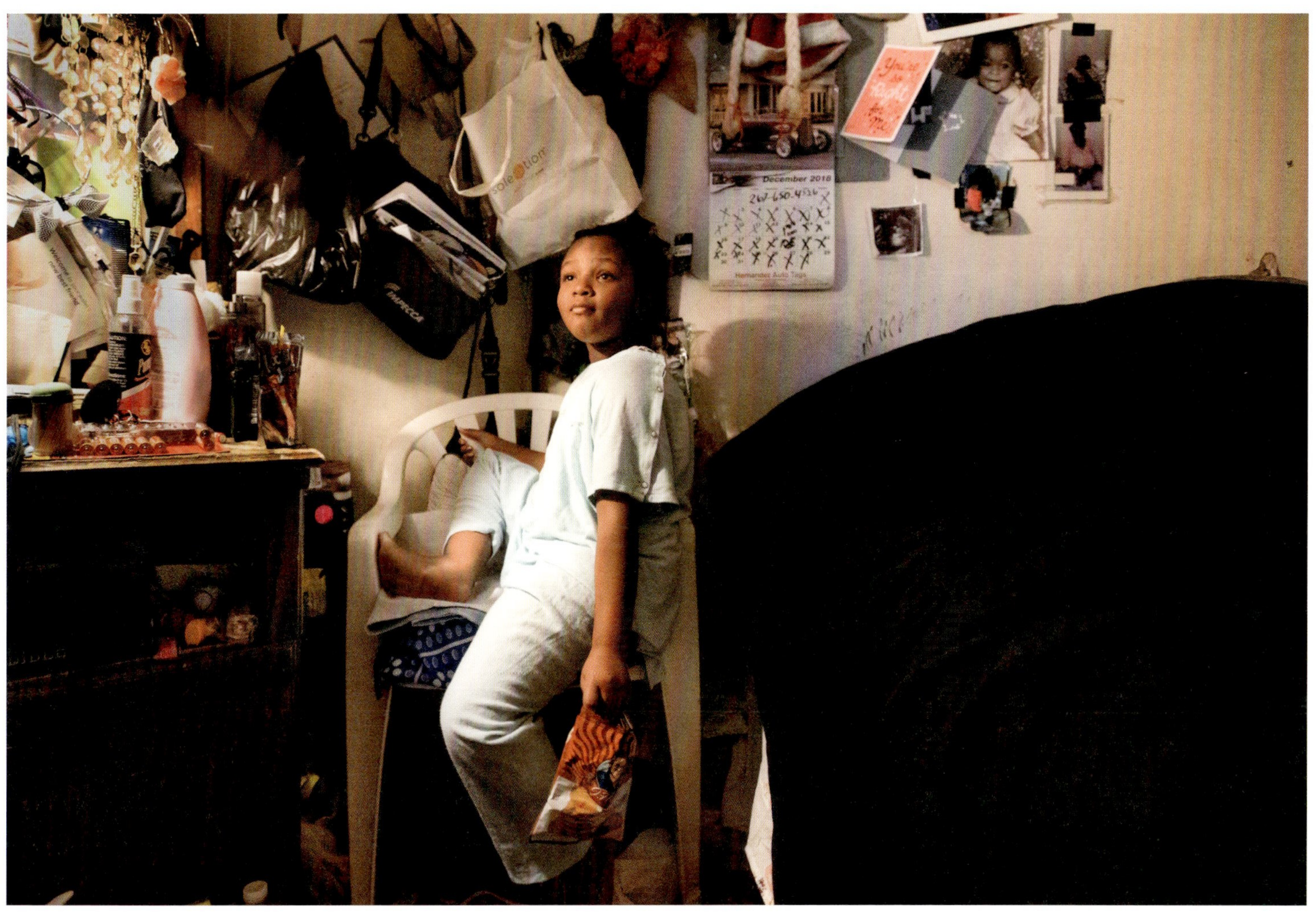

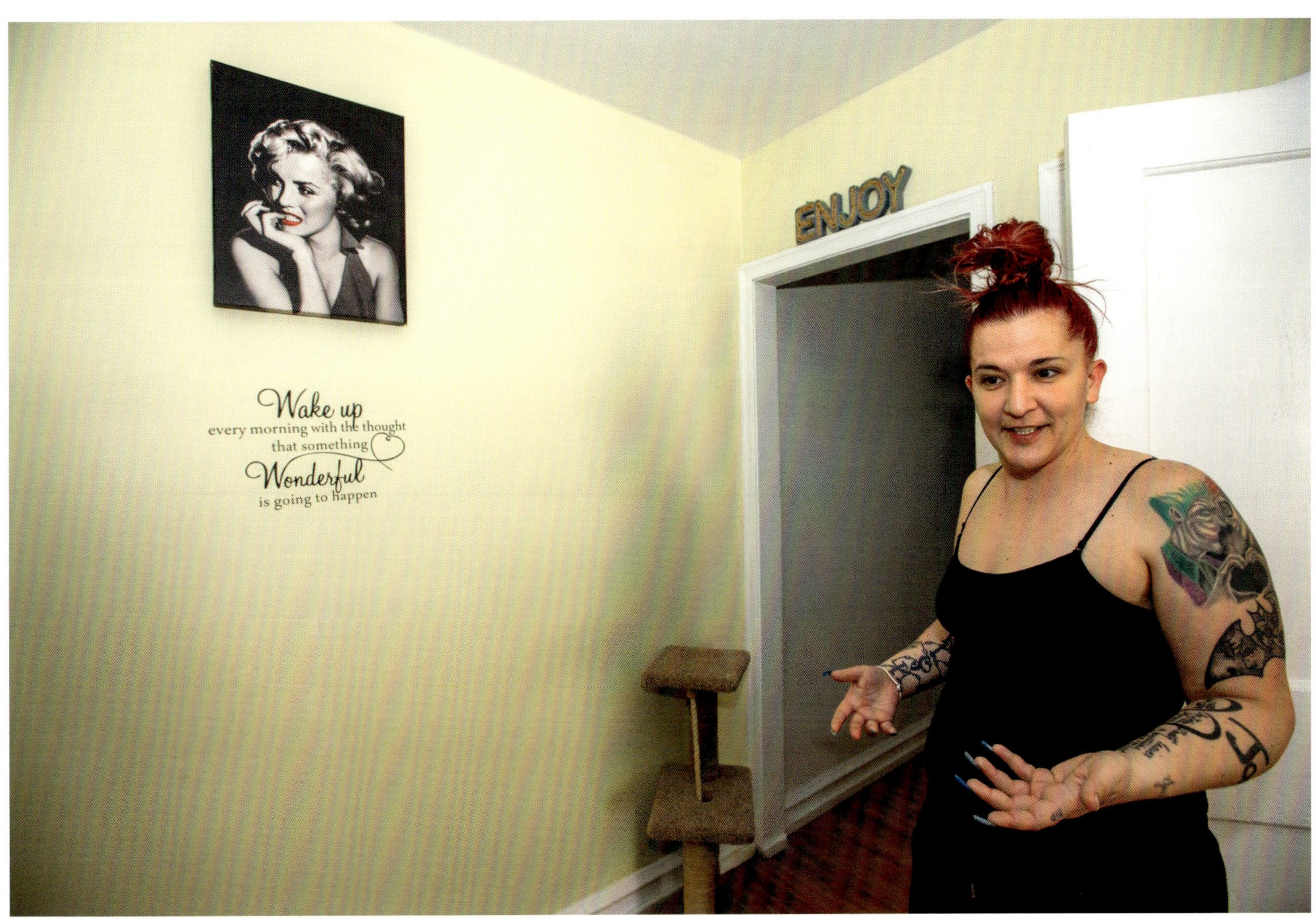
ENJOY
Wake up
every morning with the thought
that something
Wonderful
is going to happen

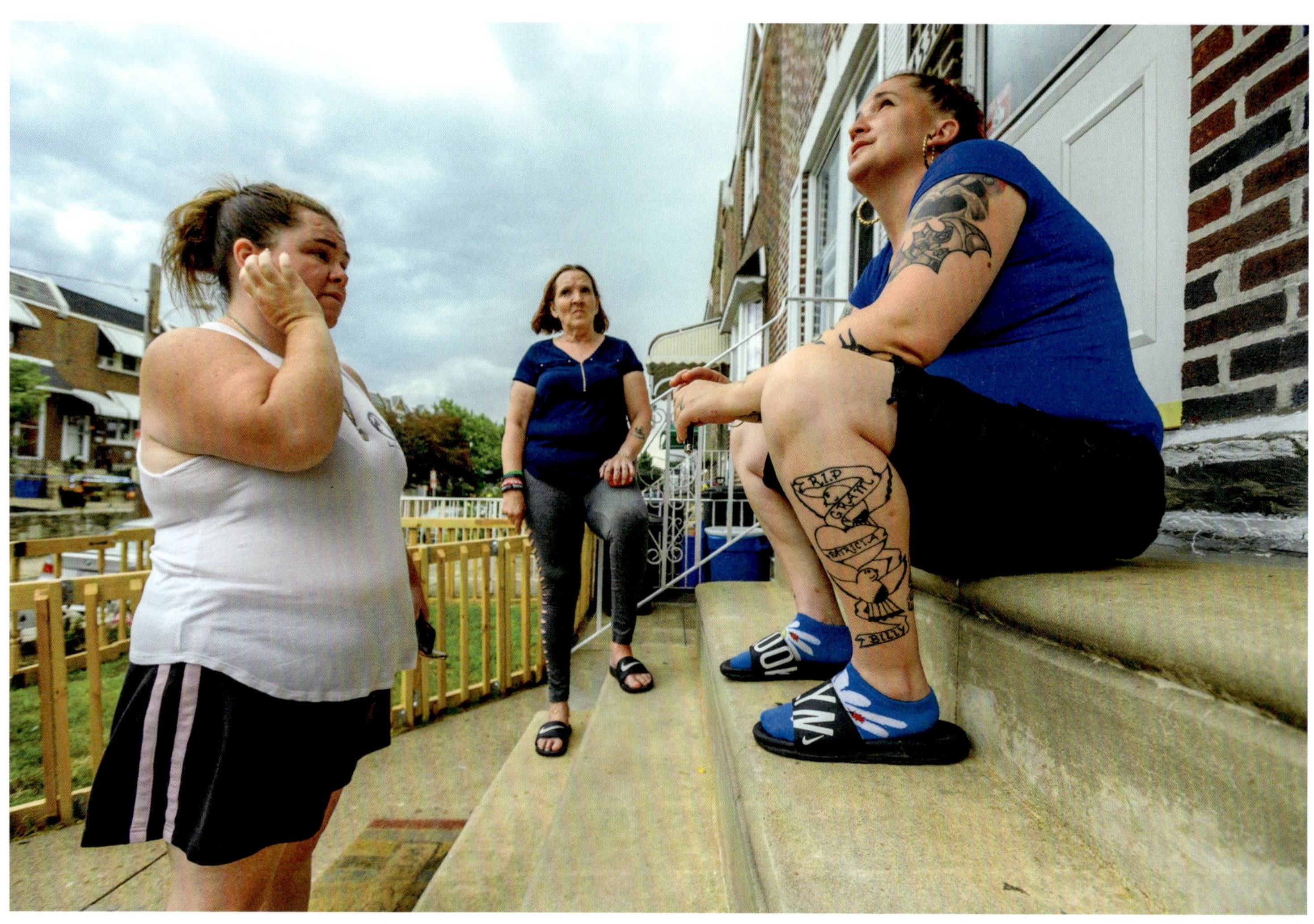

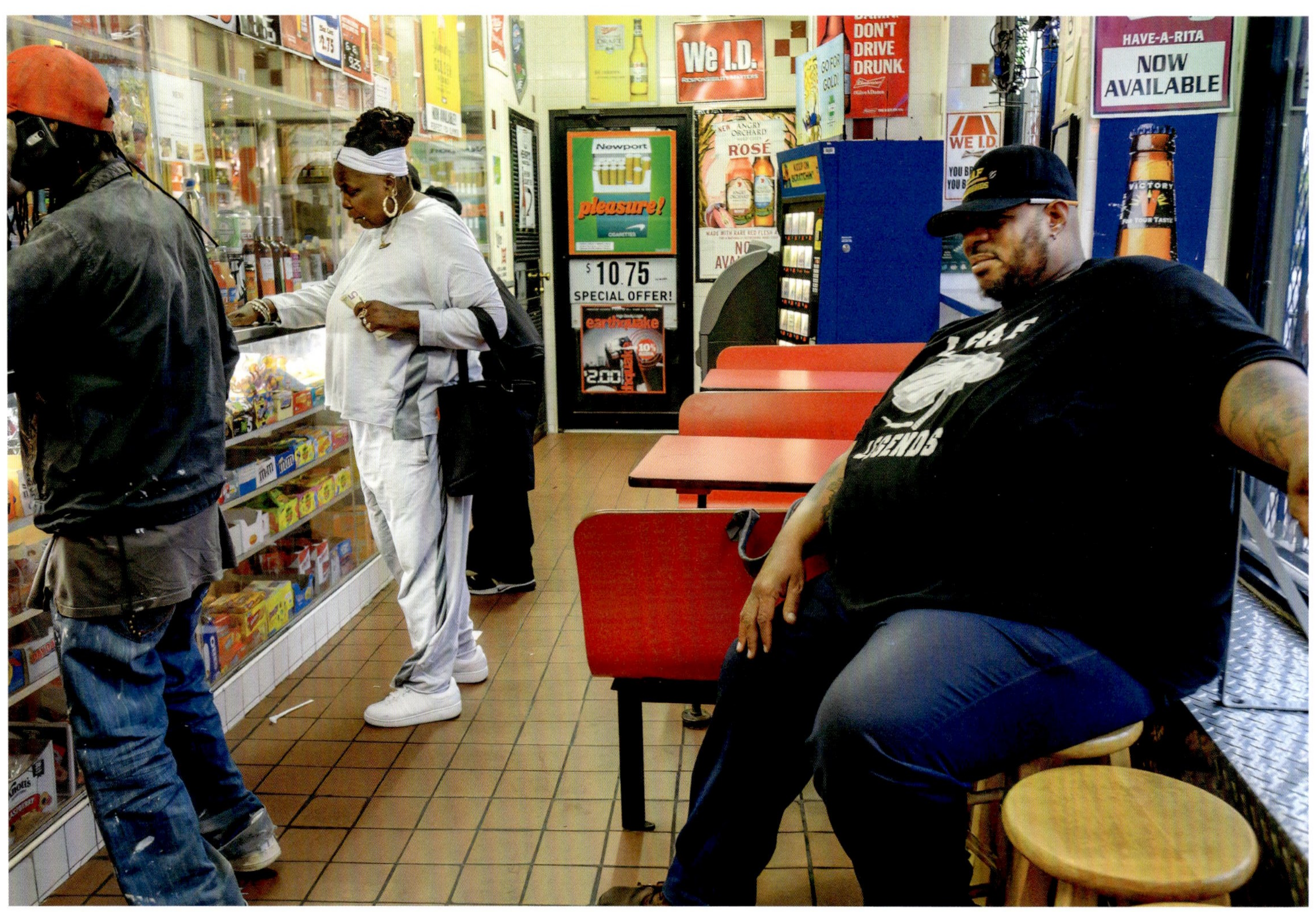

HAVE-A-RITA
NOW
AVAILABLE
We I.D.
DON'T
DRIVE
DRUNK.
Newport
pleasure!
ROSÉ
WE I.D.
$ 10.75
SPECIAL OFFER!
earthquake
200
VICTORY
LEGENDS

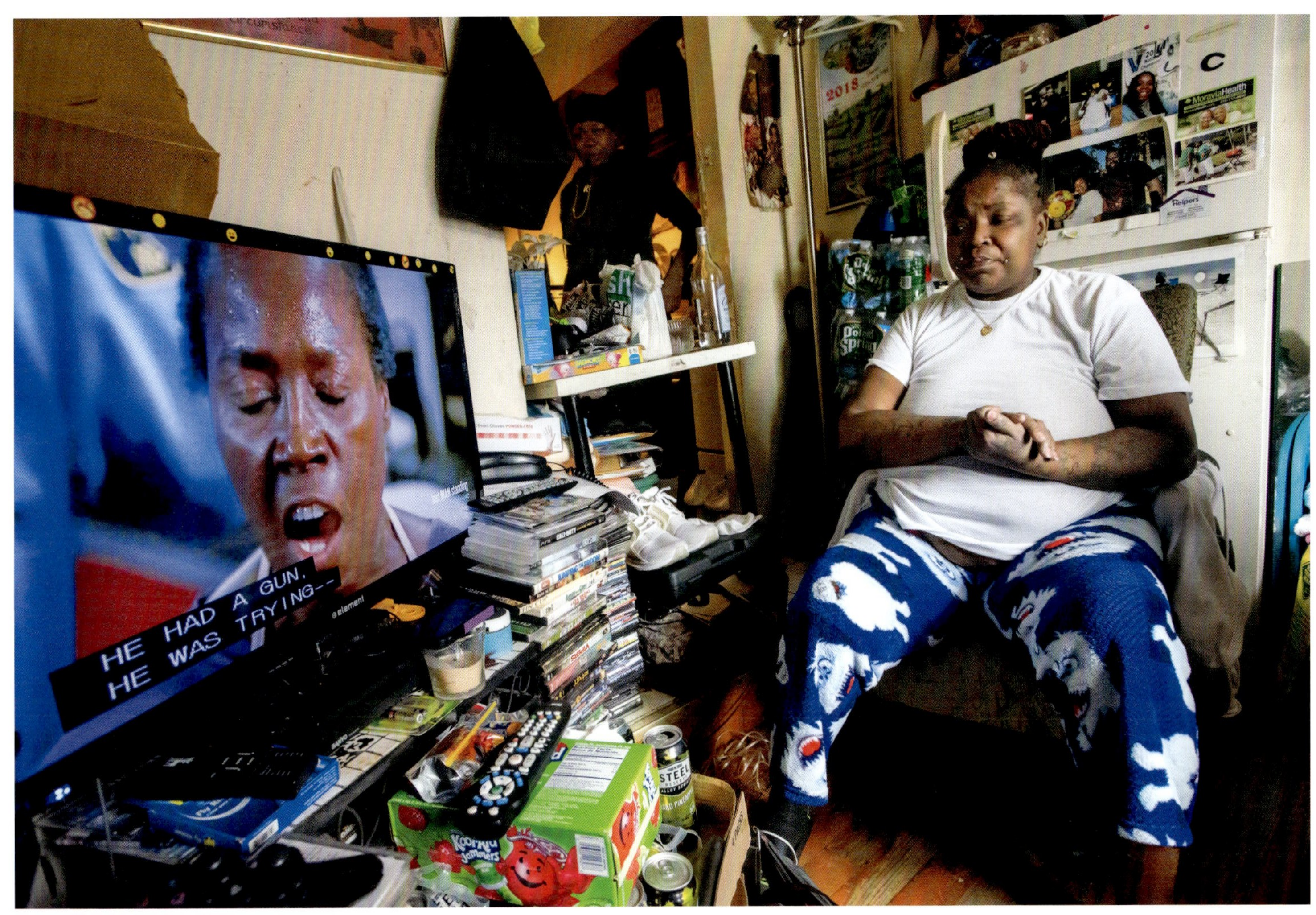
HE HAD A GUN,
HE WAS TRYING--

"Who that? OK. Well, let him know. That's not fair. He's a woman beater. He beat my daughter in front of my grandkids. I'm on my way, dog. I'm on my way. Ain't no real man going to beat their woman in front of nobody. That ain't respect. That ain't no respect."

"You're a woman beater, dog. She feed you. That's bullshit. Get the hell out of there. I done call the cops and tell them what he got. I don't give a fuck. Call me a snitch. He got that gun in that backpack."

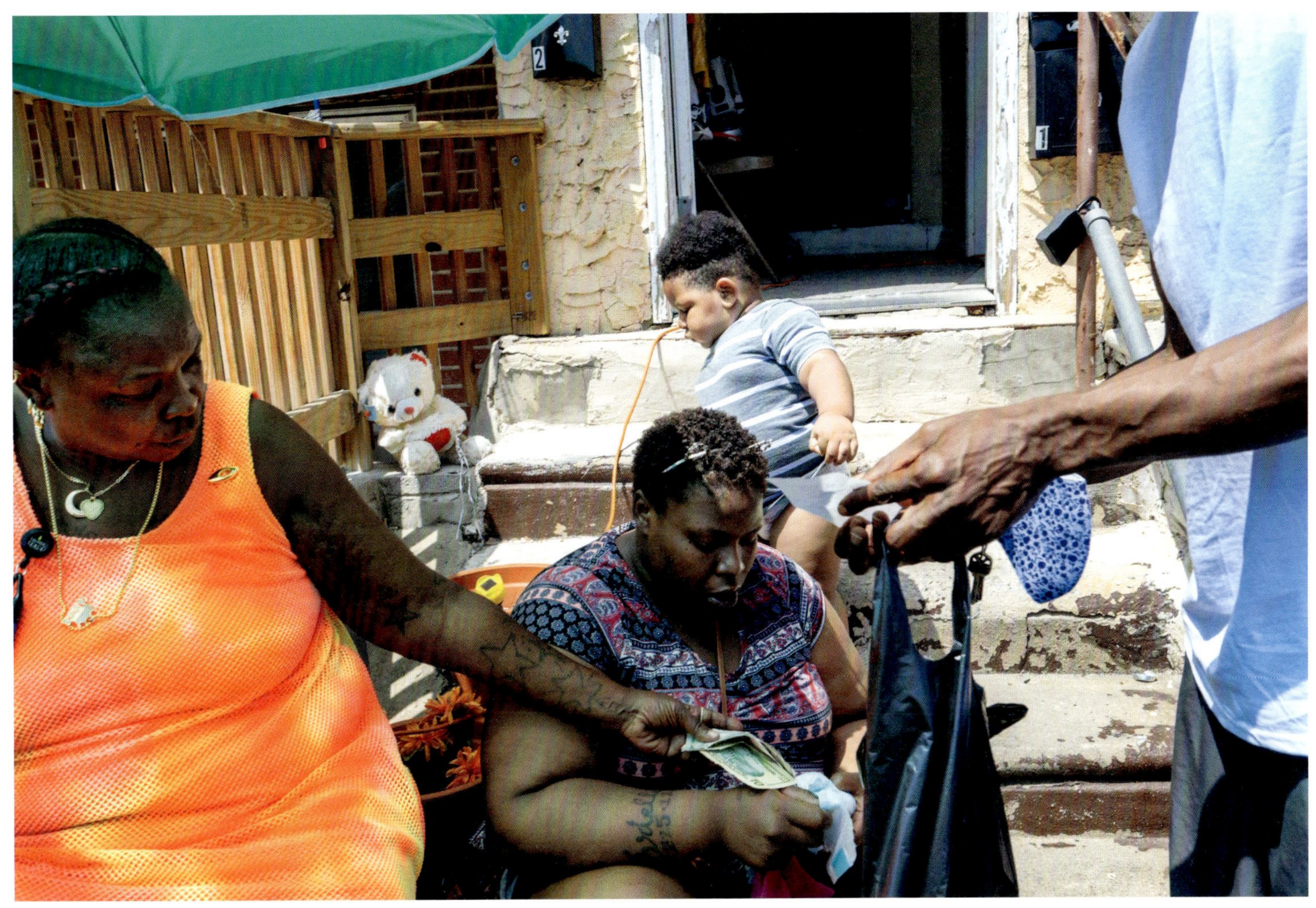

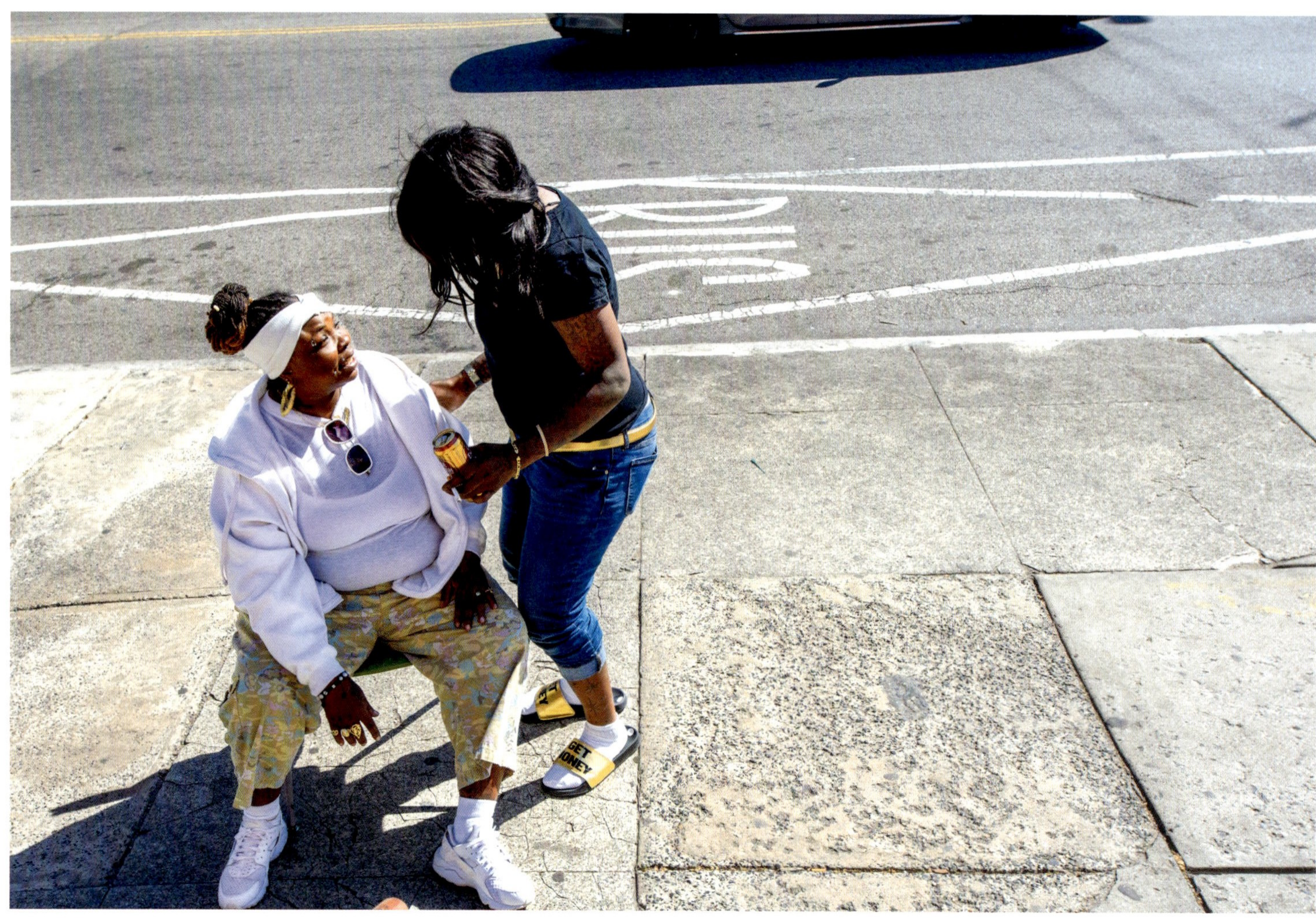

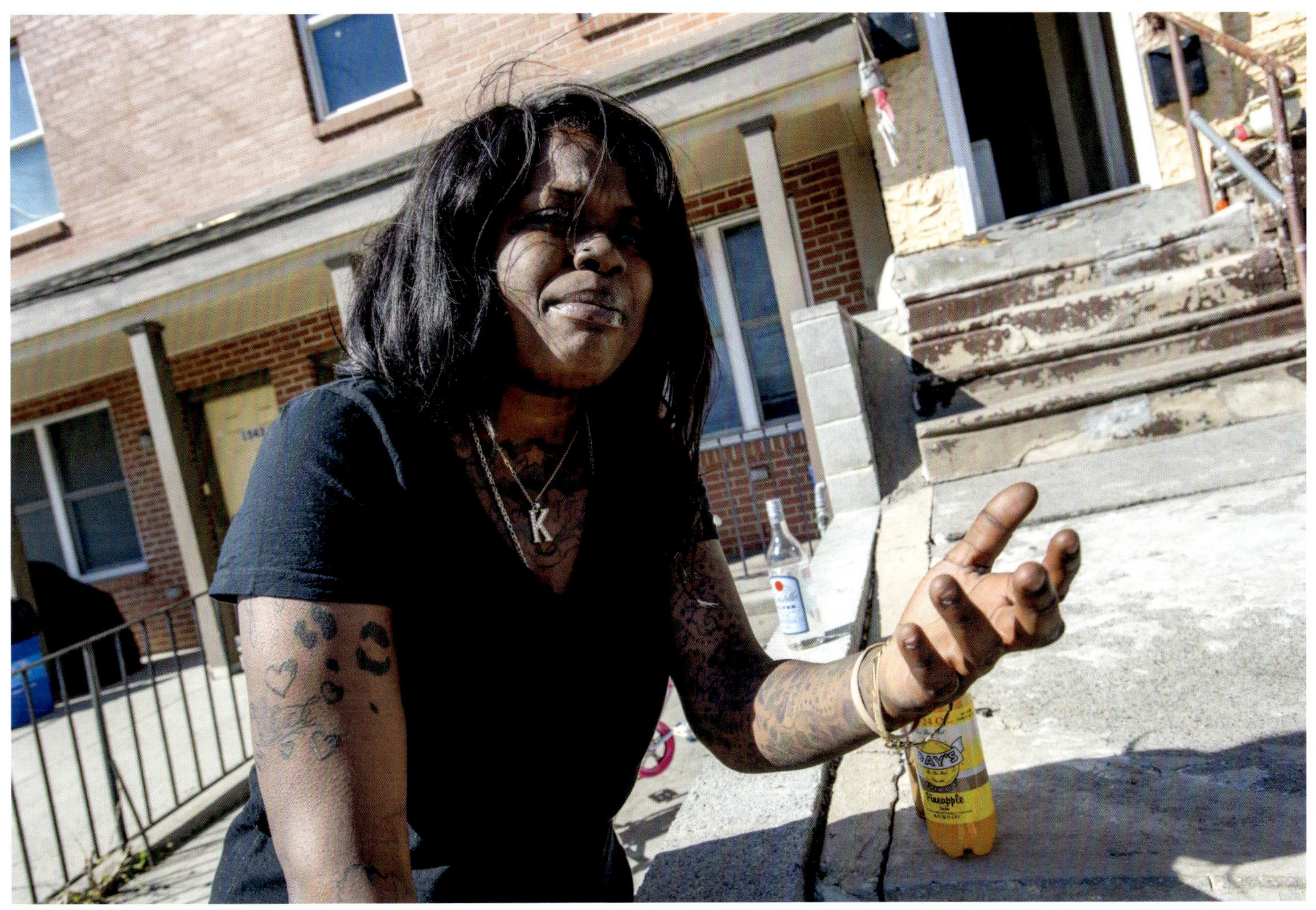

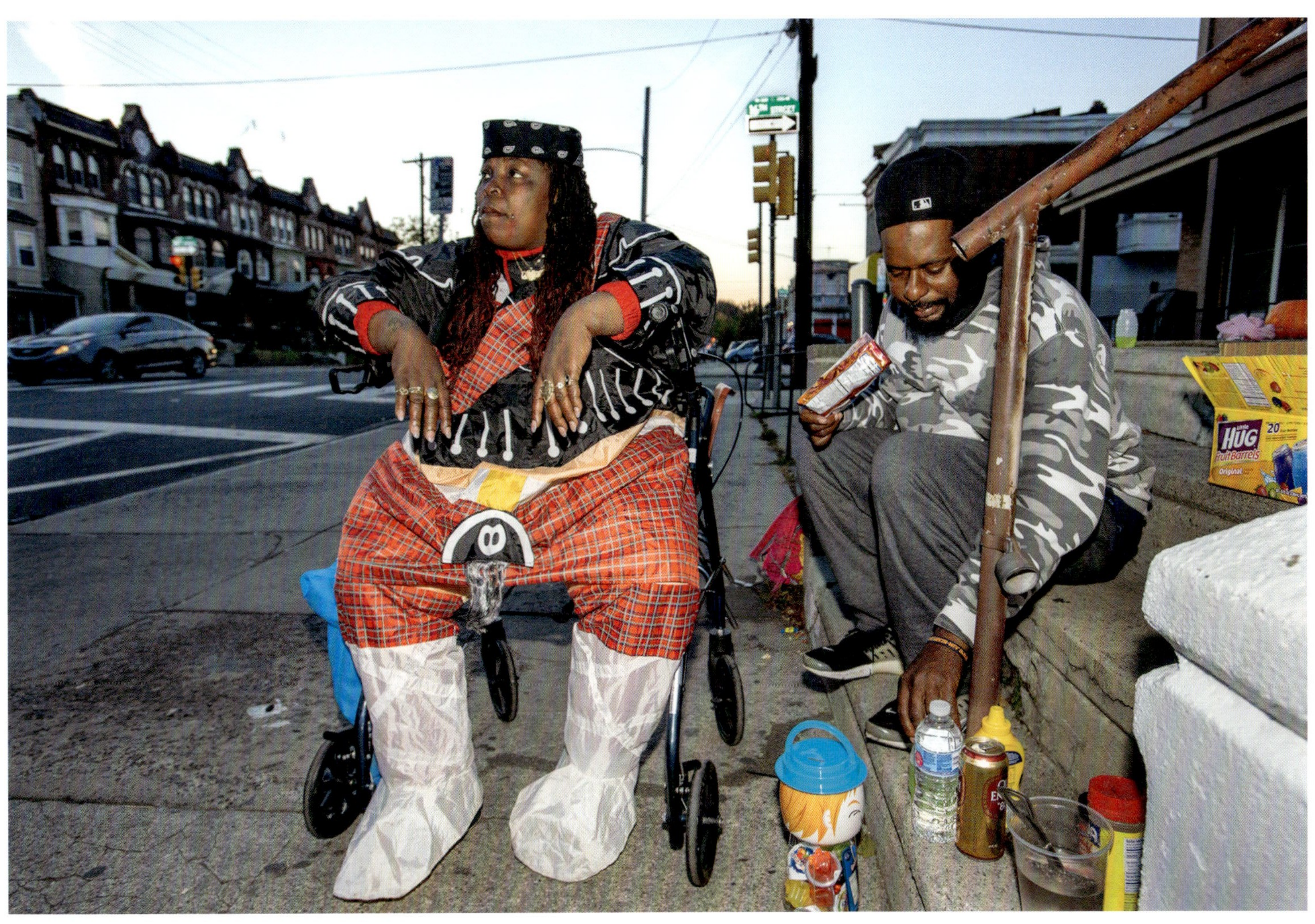

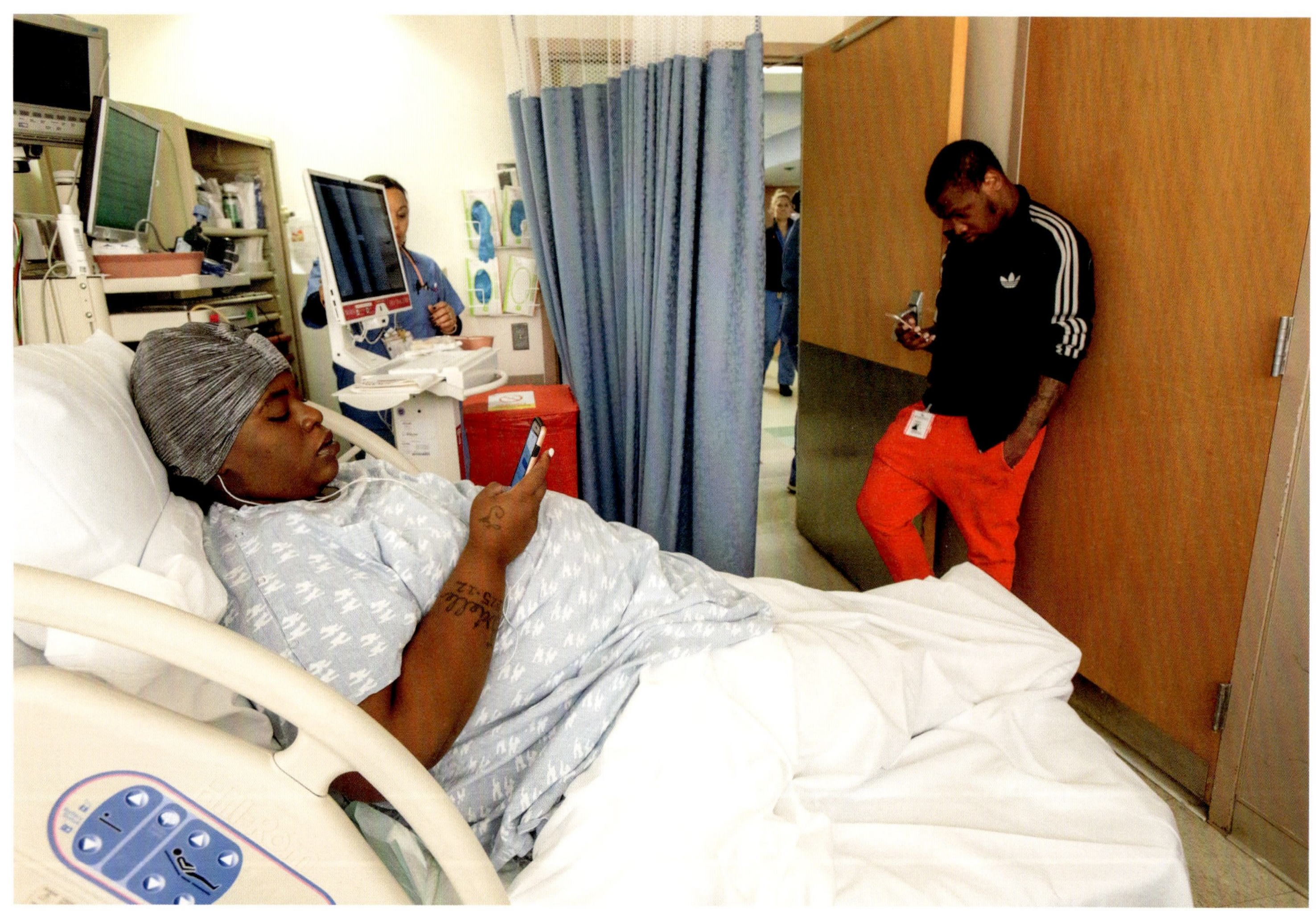

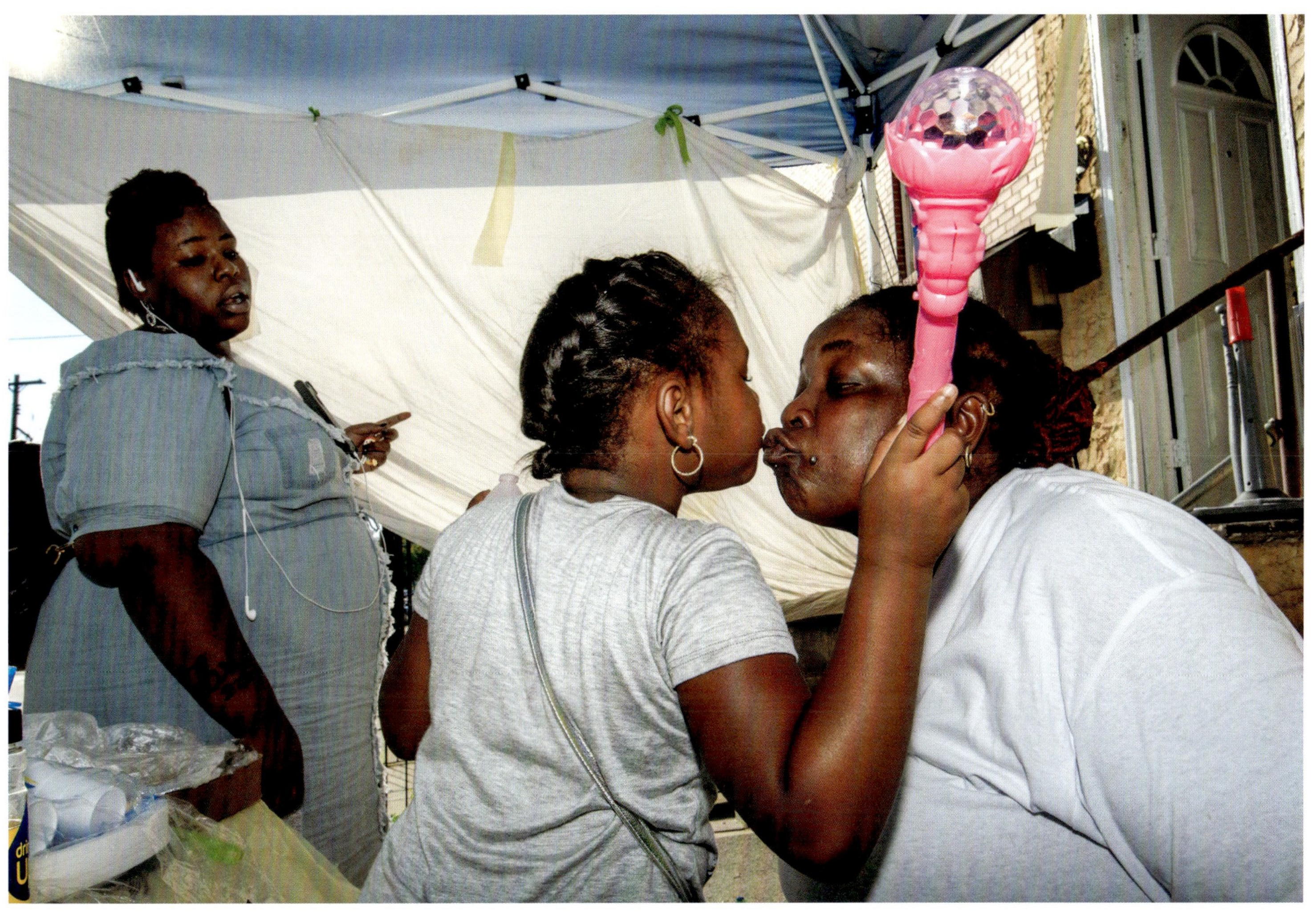

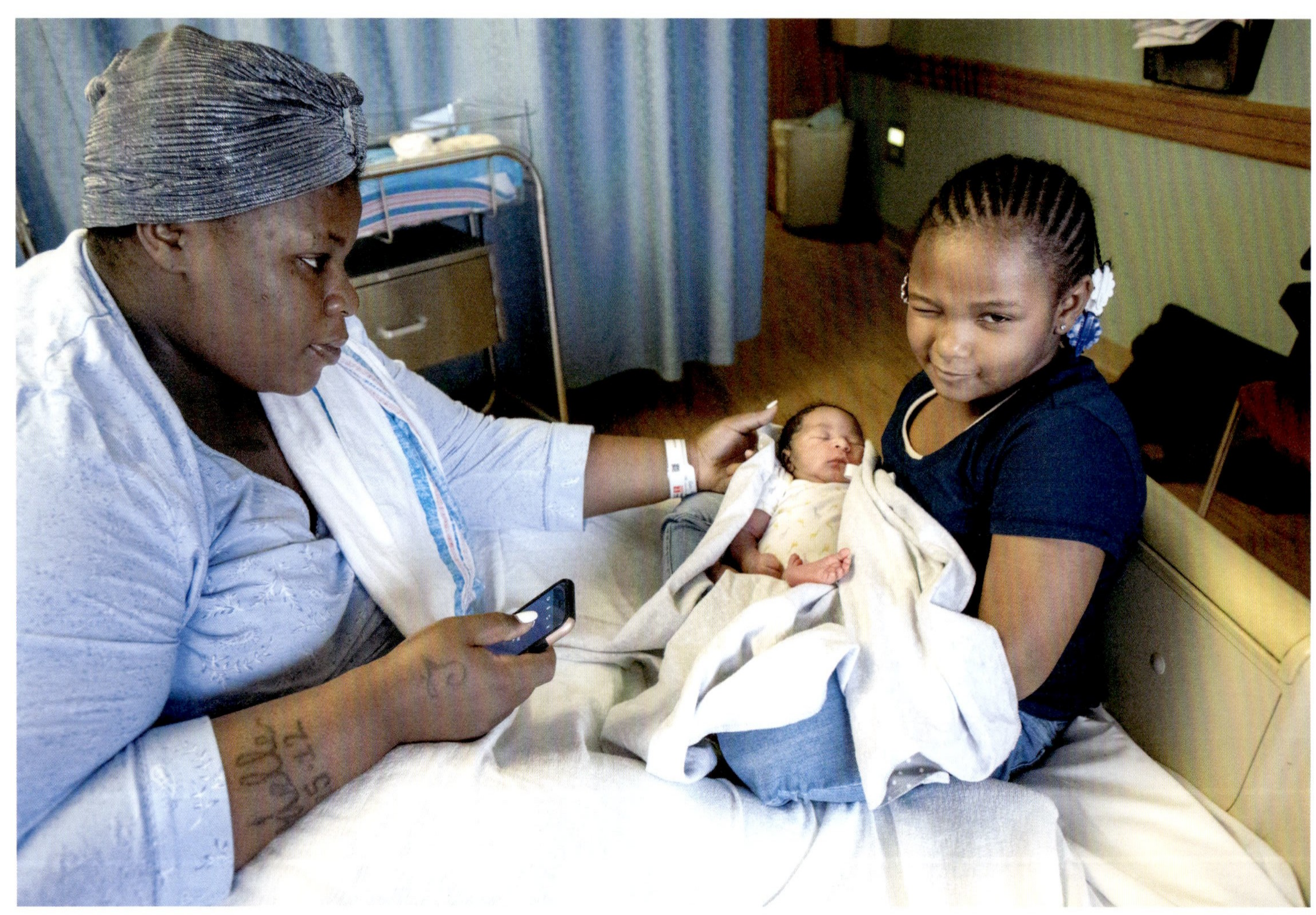

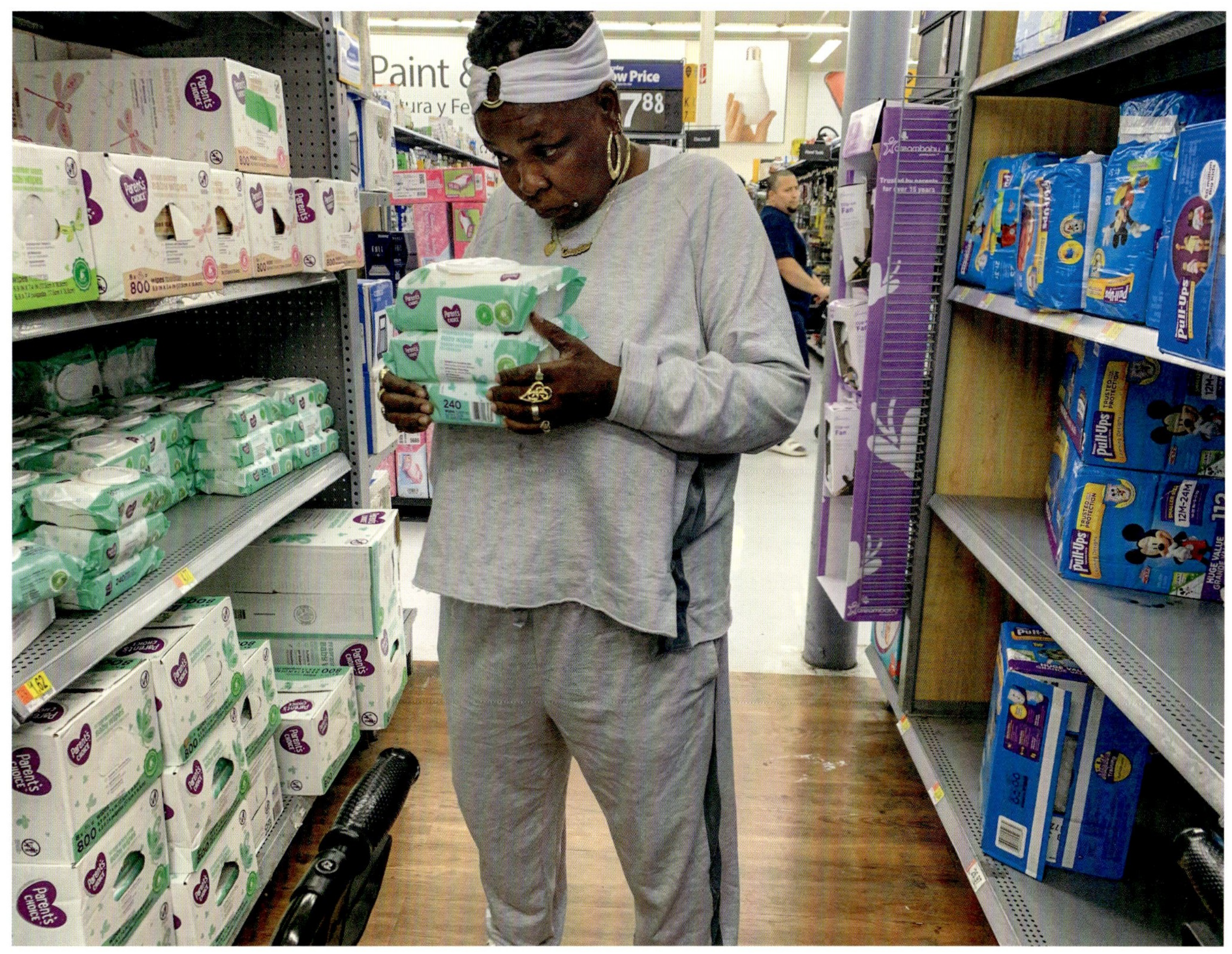

Paint &
ra y Fe
w Price
7 88
Parent's choice
800
Parent's choice
800
240
Pull-Ups
Pull-Ups
112

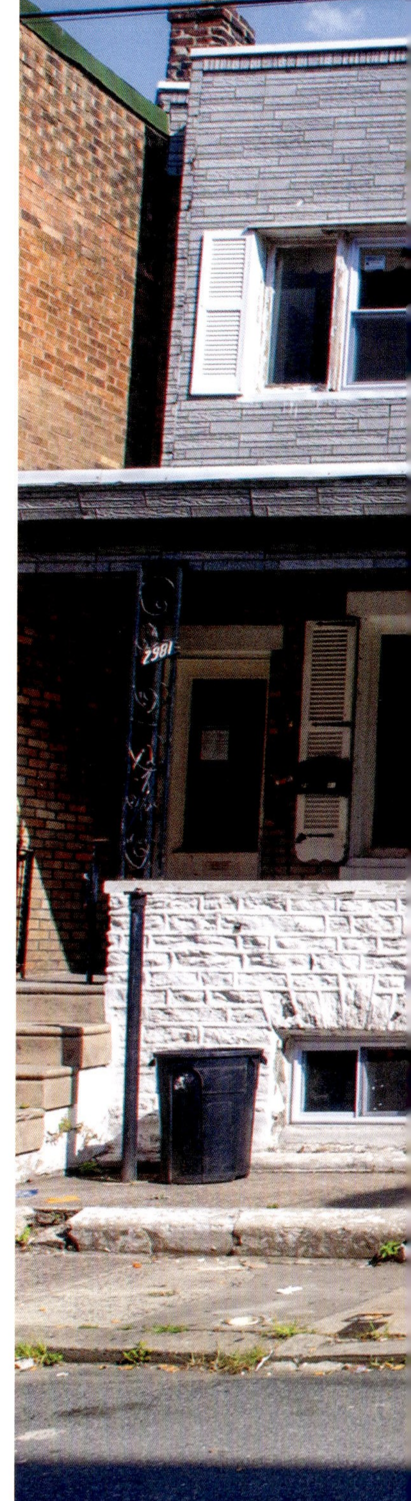

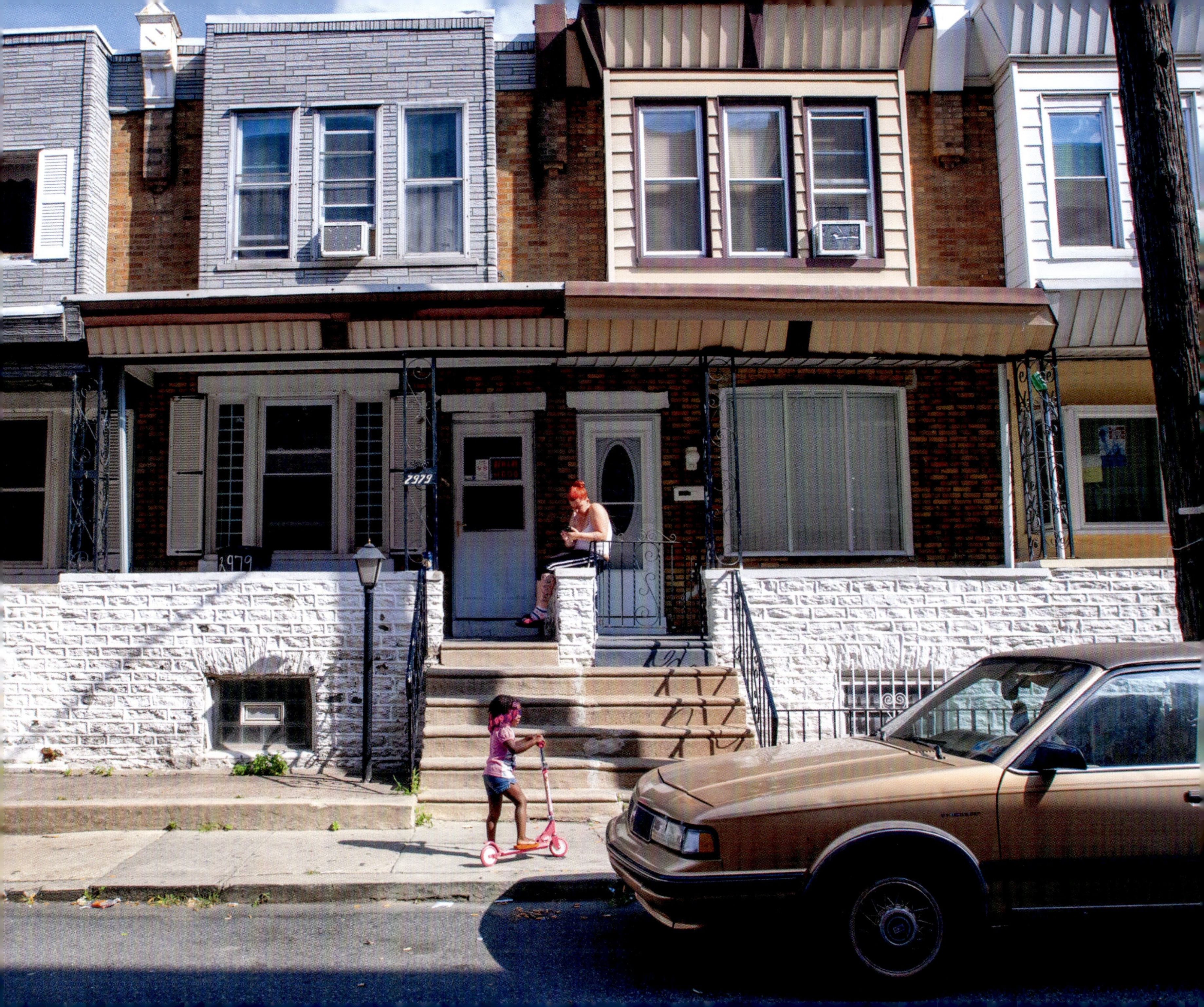

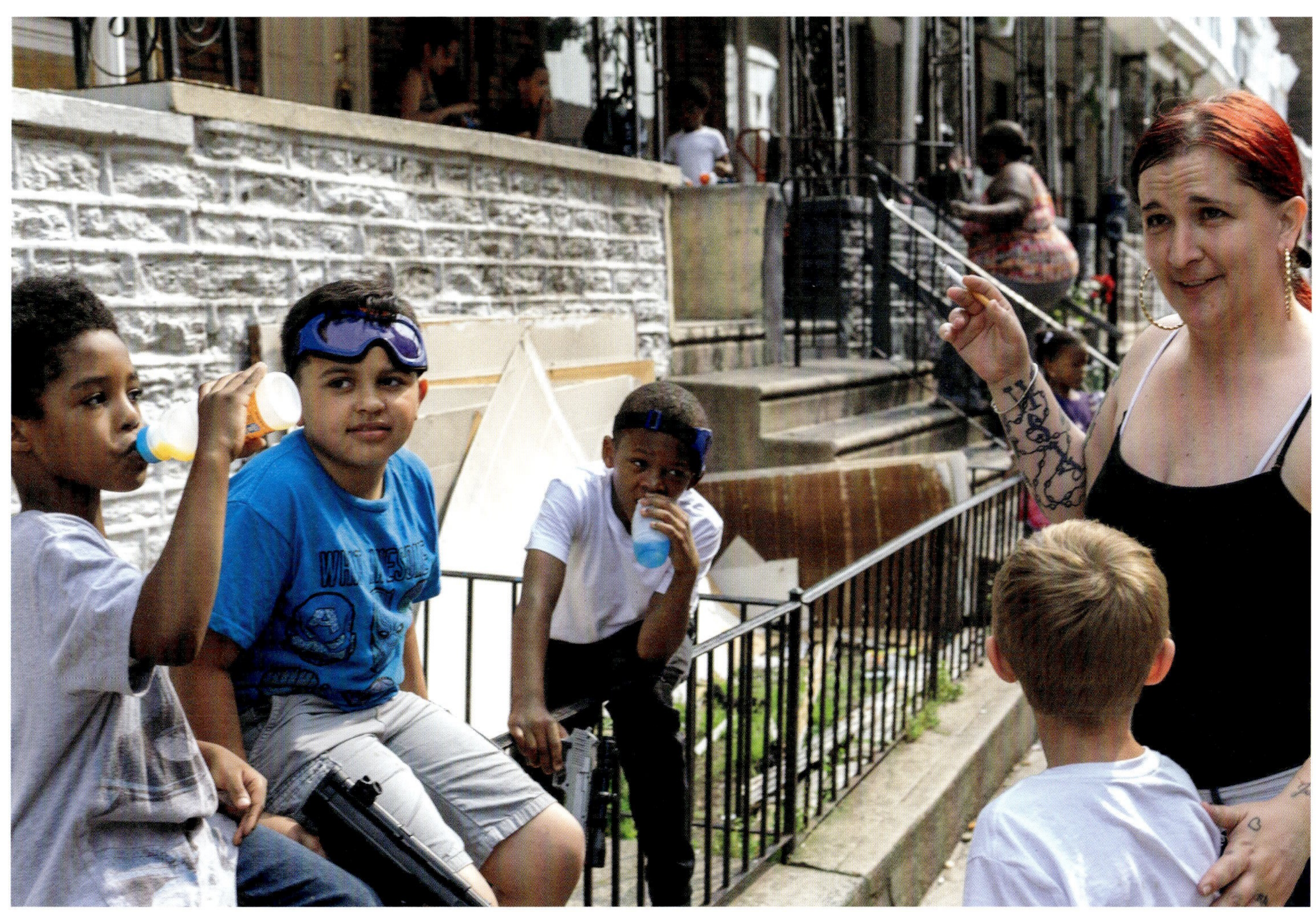

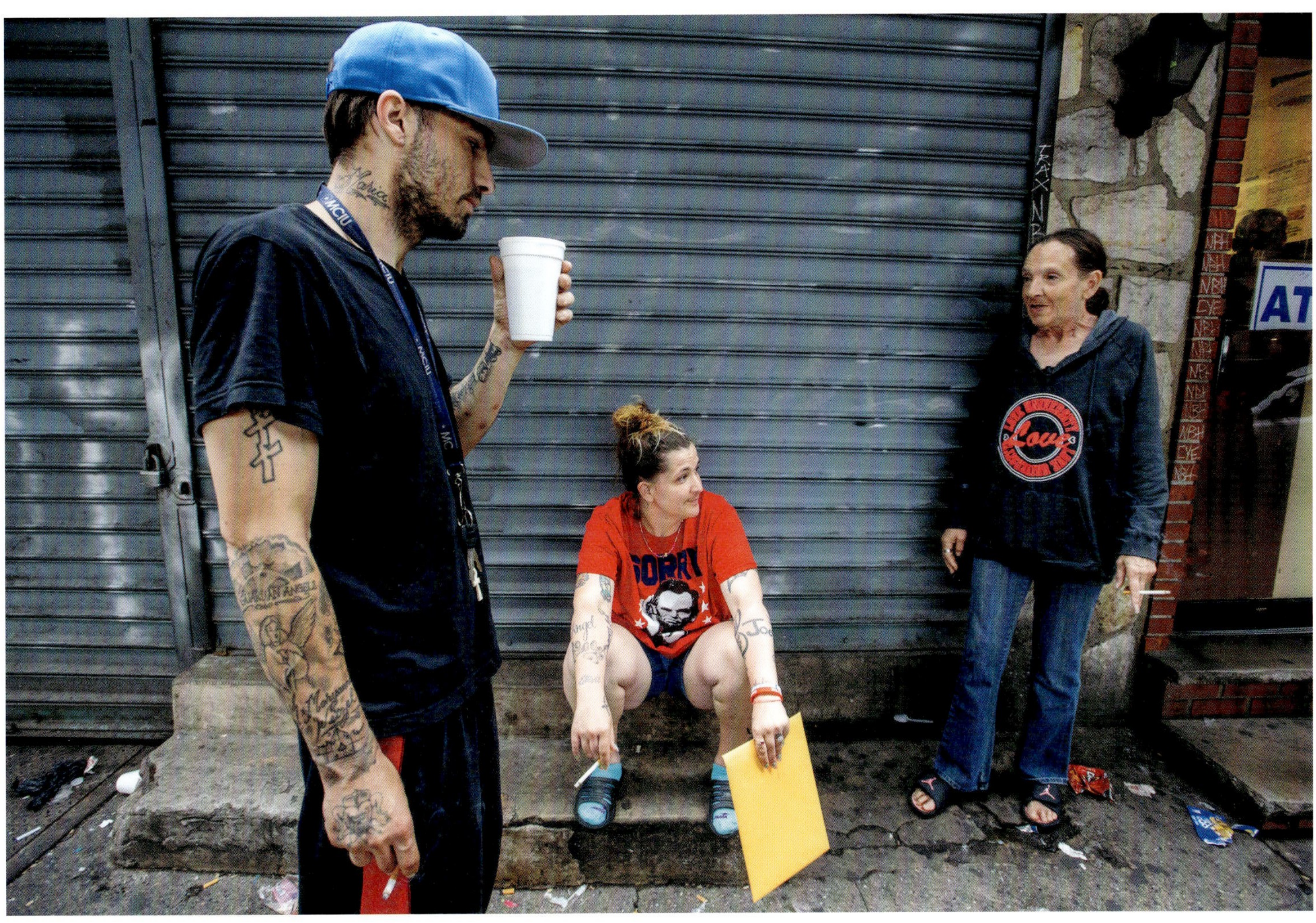

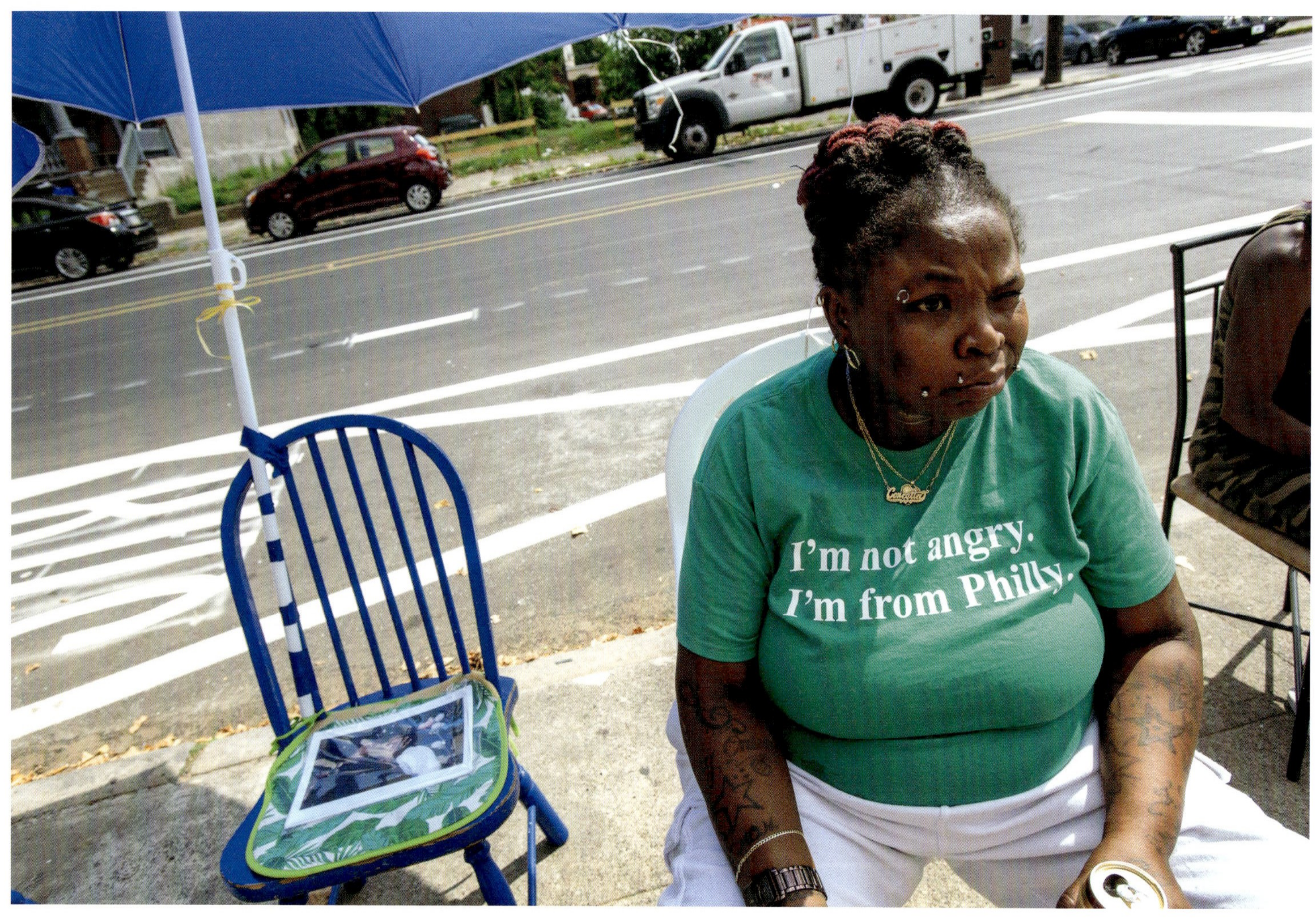

"Green Eyes was run over by an off-duty cop. He never hurt anyone. He just sold his stuff from a grocery cart on the corner. No one cares. He was just another homeless guy."

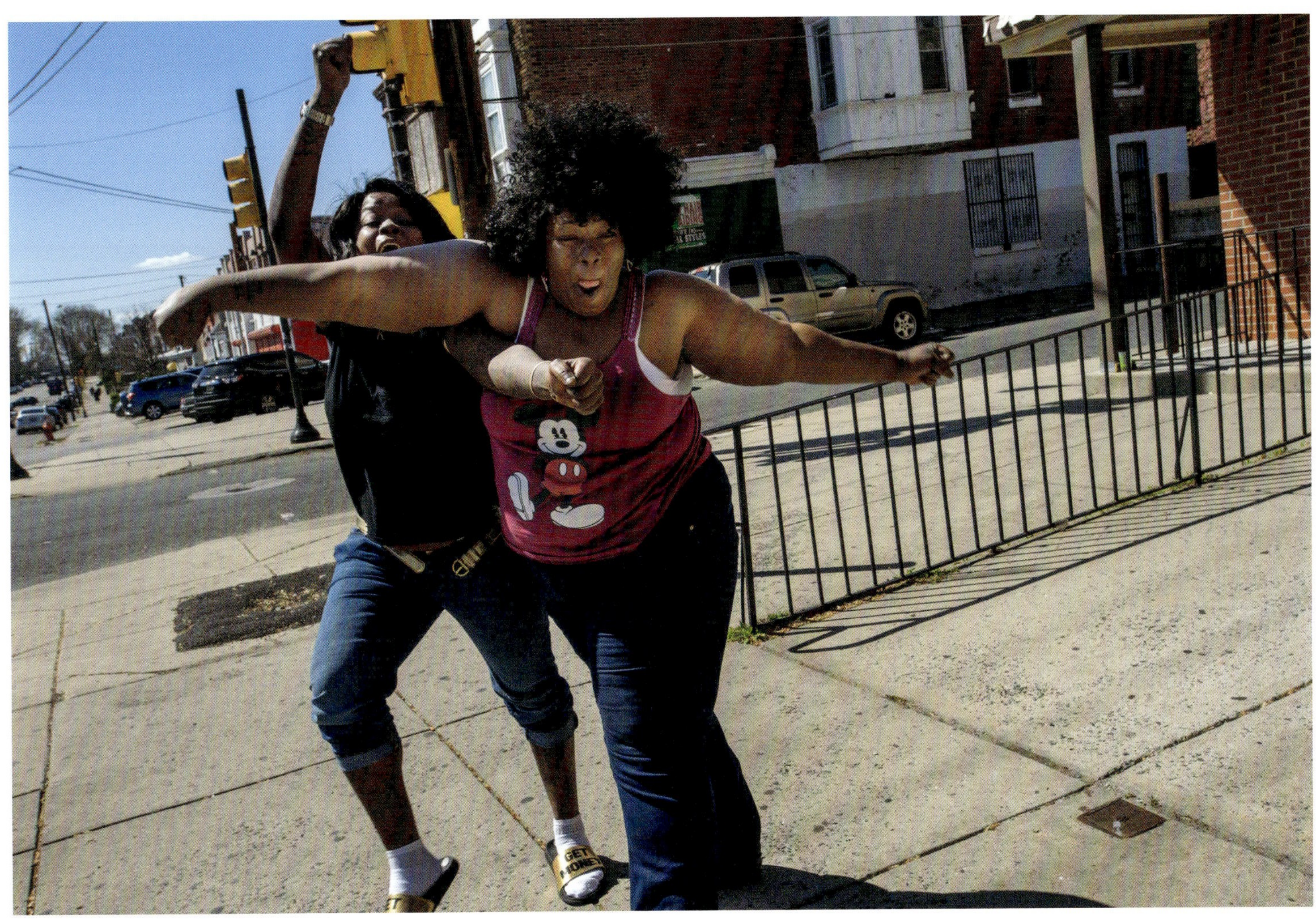

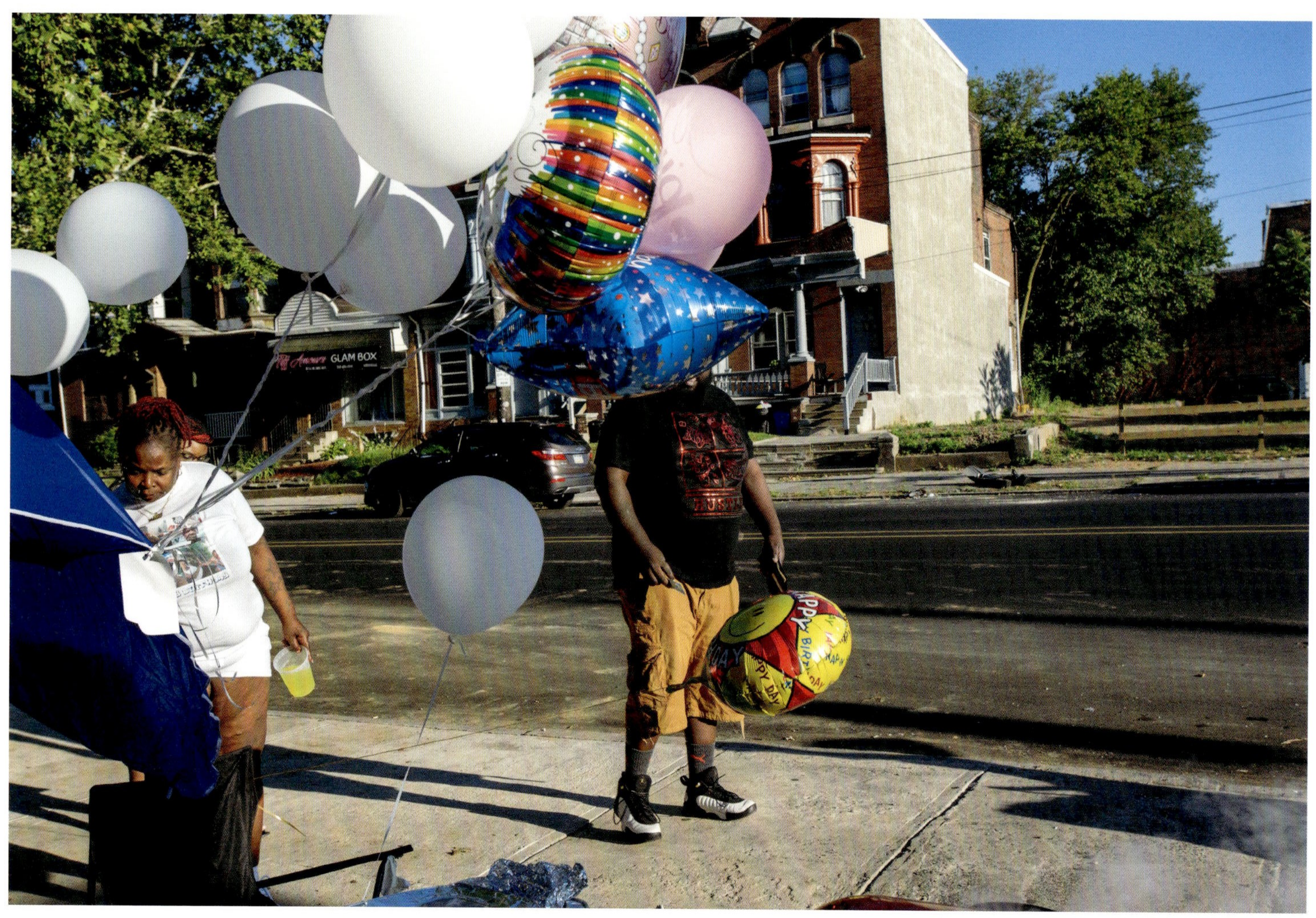

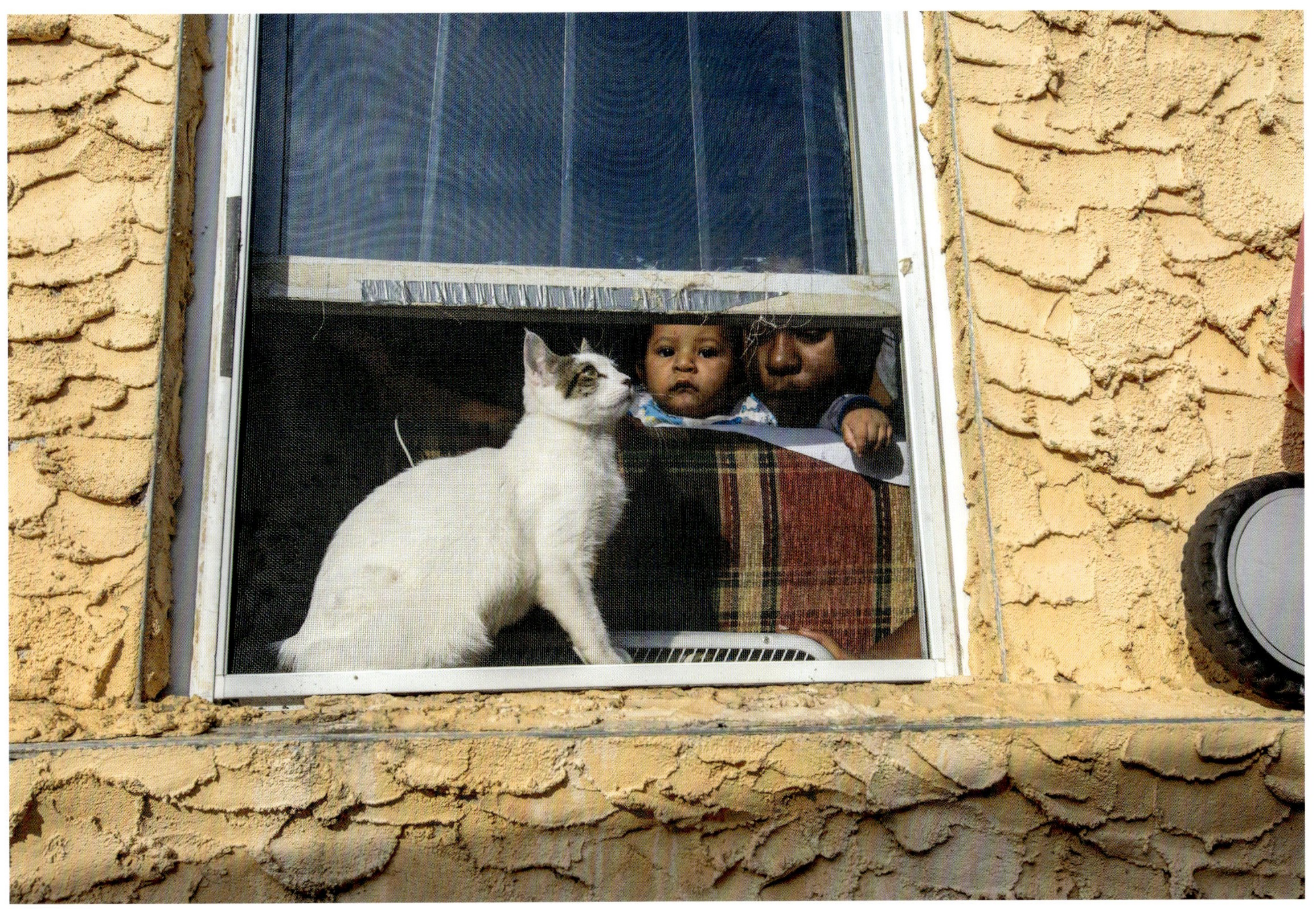

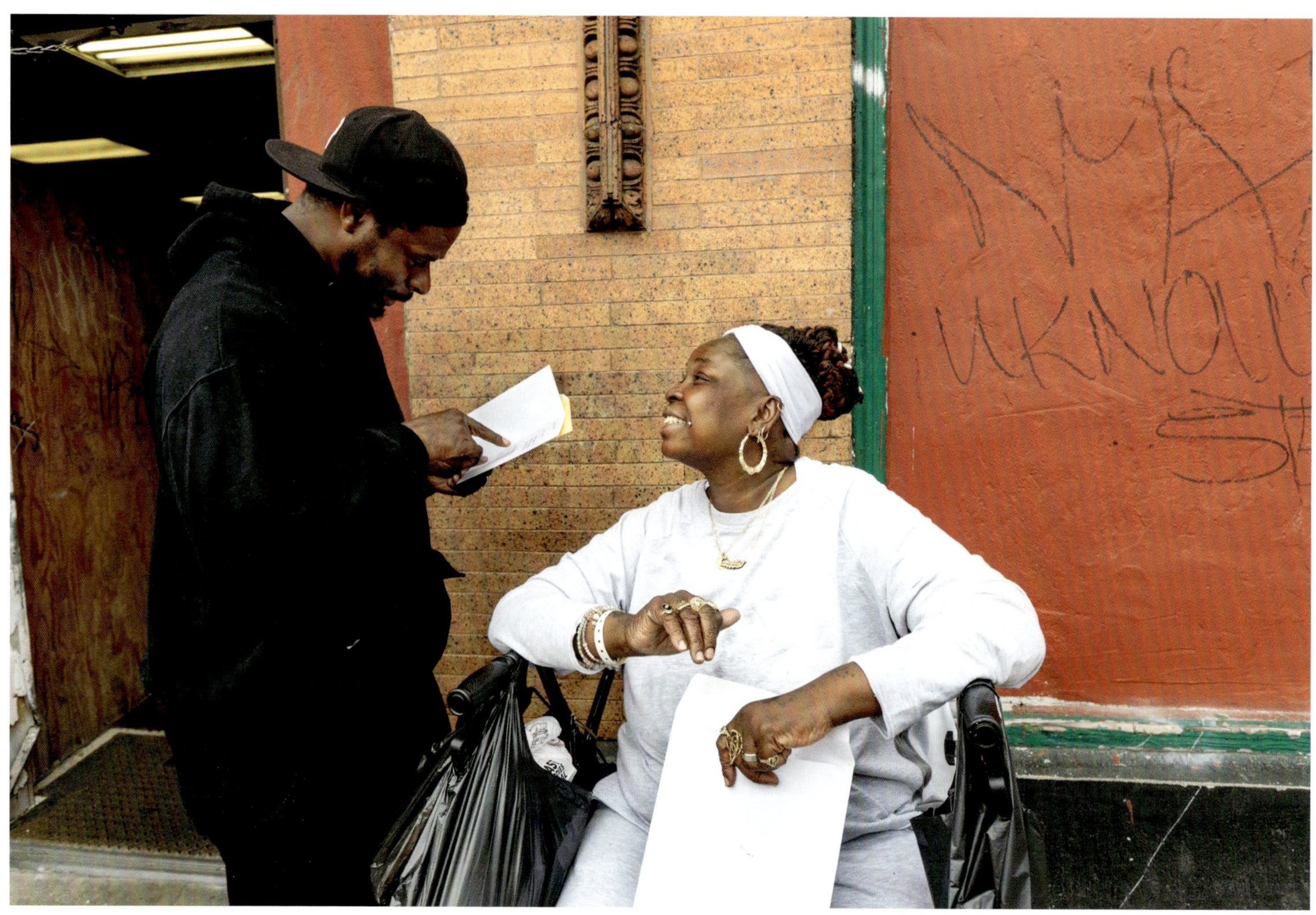

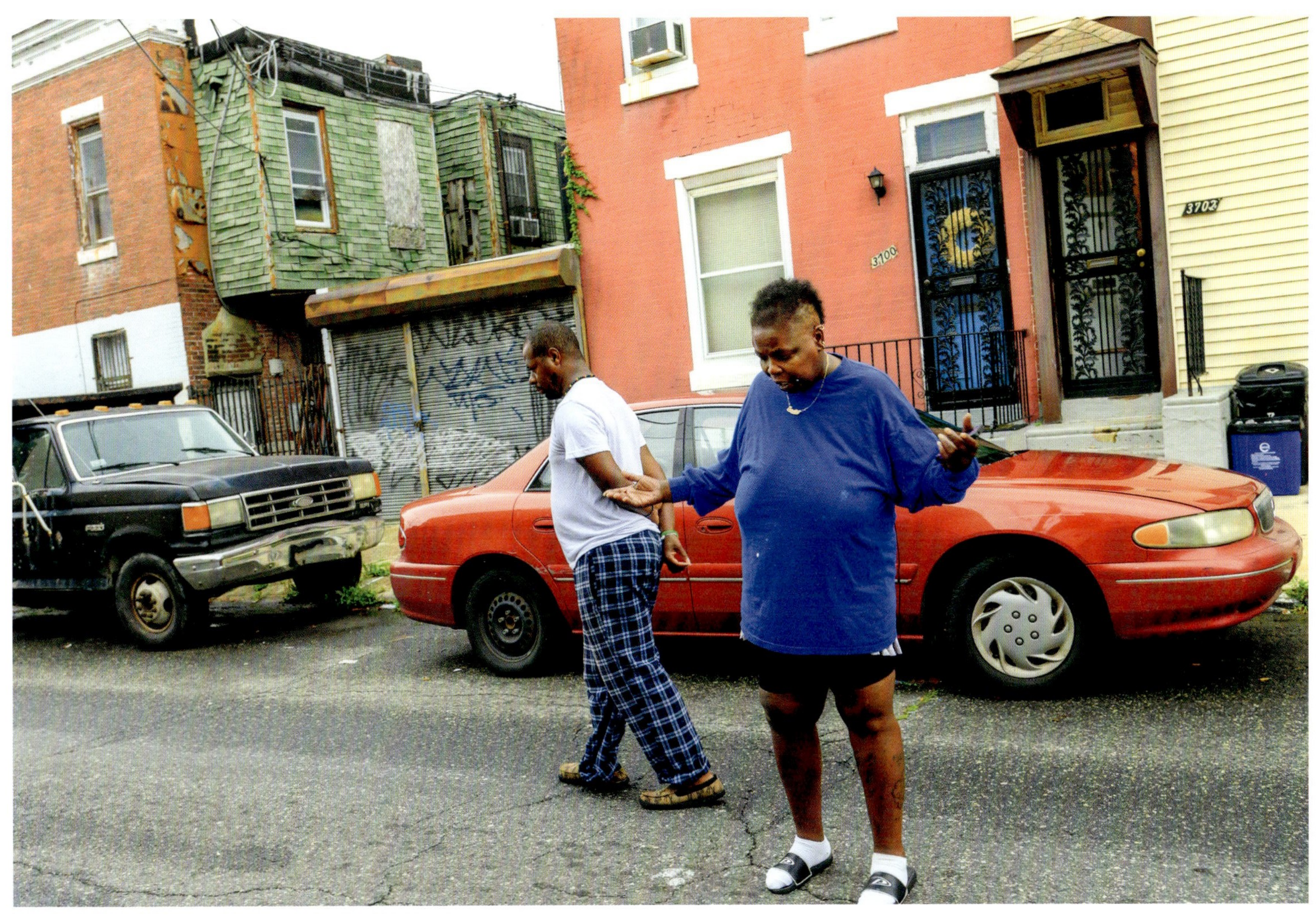

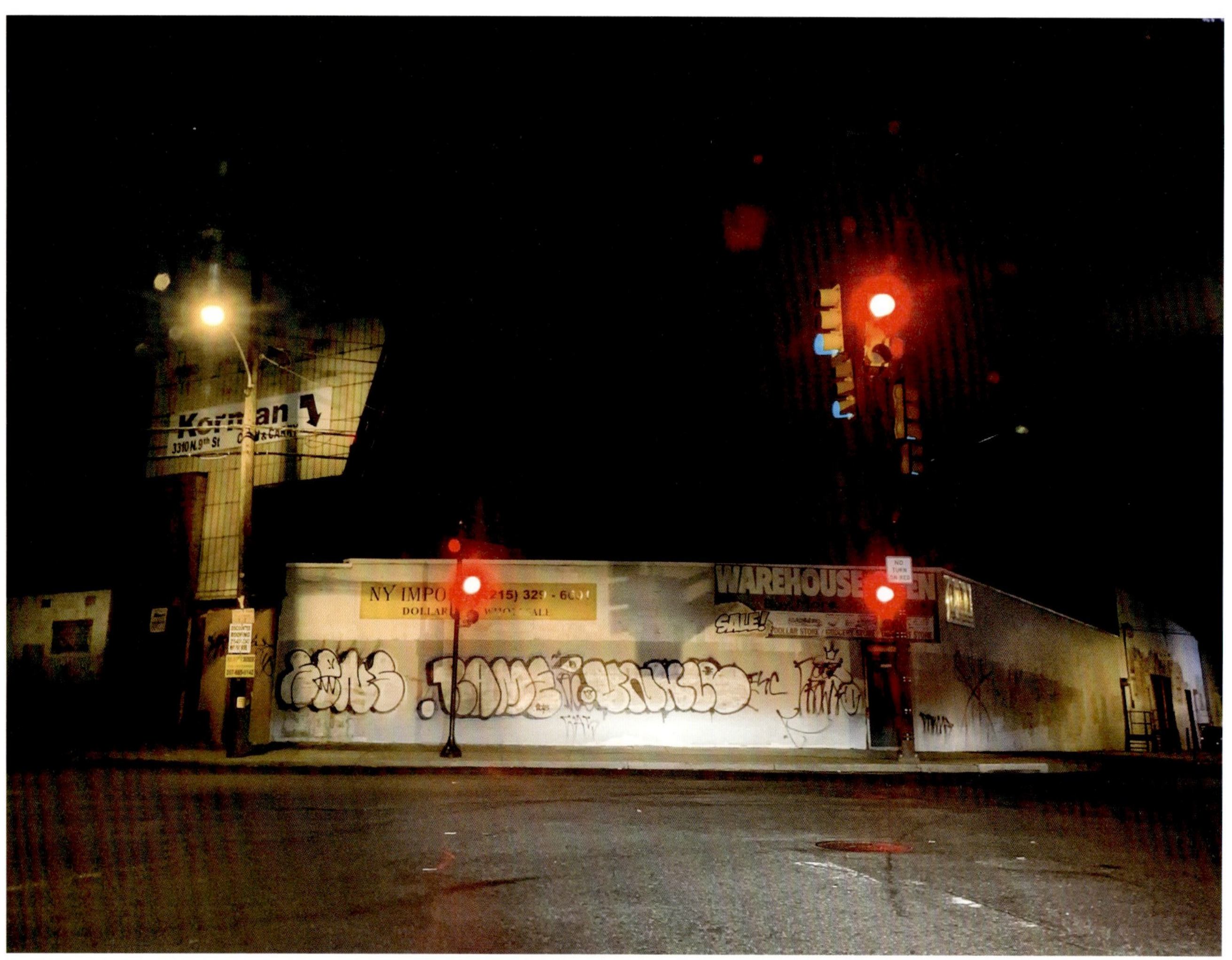

Korman
3310 N. 9th St
CASH & CARRY
NY IMPO... (215) 329 - 6000
DOLLAR... WHOLESALE
WAREHOUSE...EN

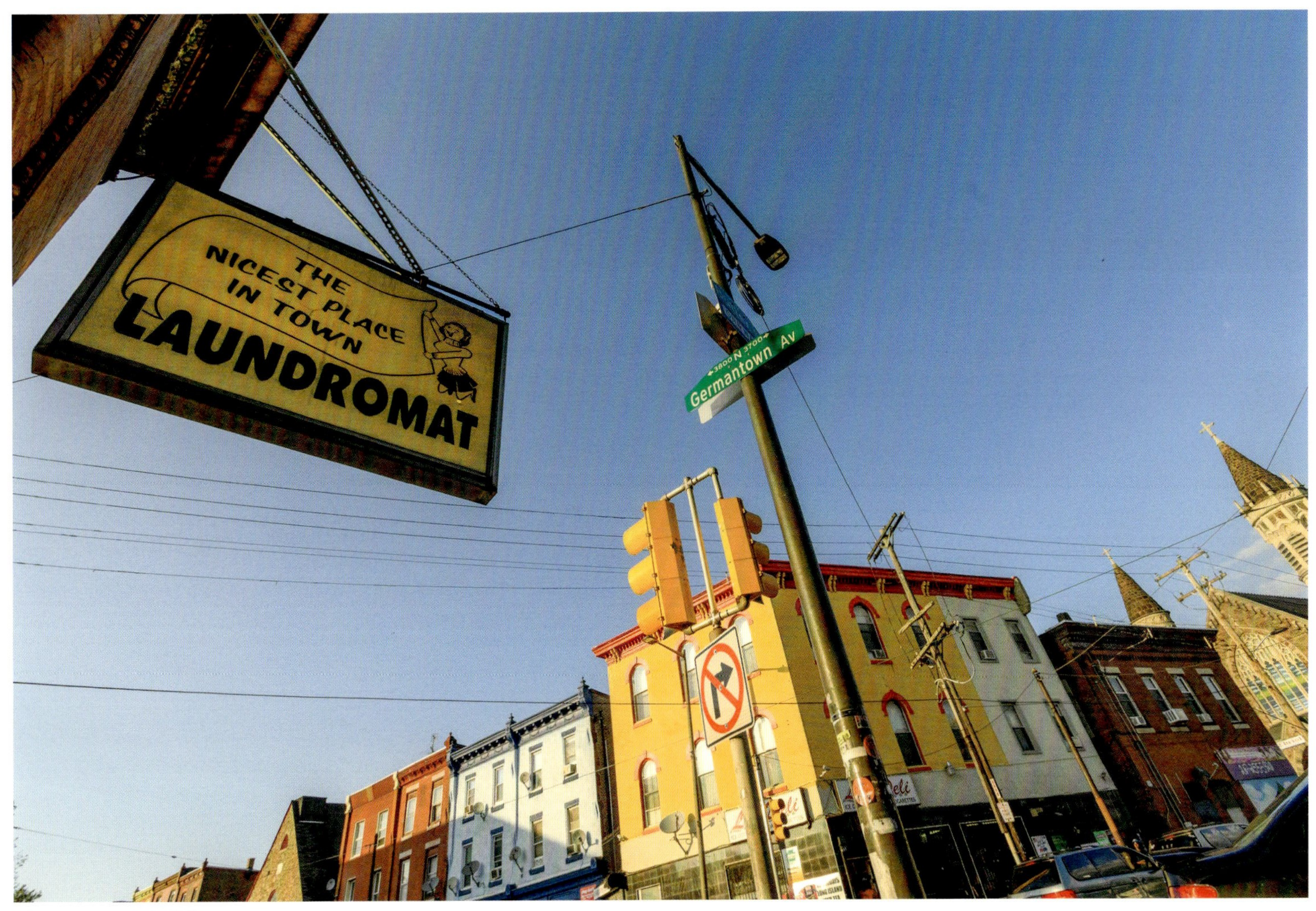
THE
NICEST PLACE
IN TOWN
LAUNDROMAT
Germantown Av

"What I eat don't make you shit. What you eat don't make me shit. Otherwise, you can love me or leave me alone.
Because if you don't love me, my Father above always will."

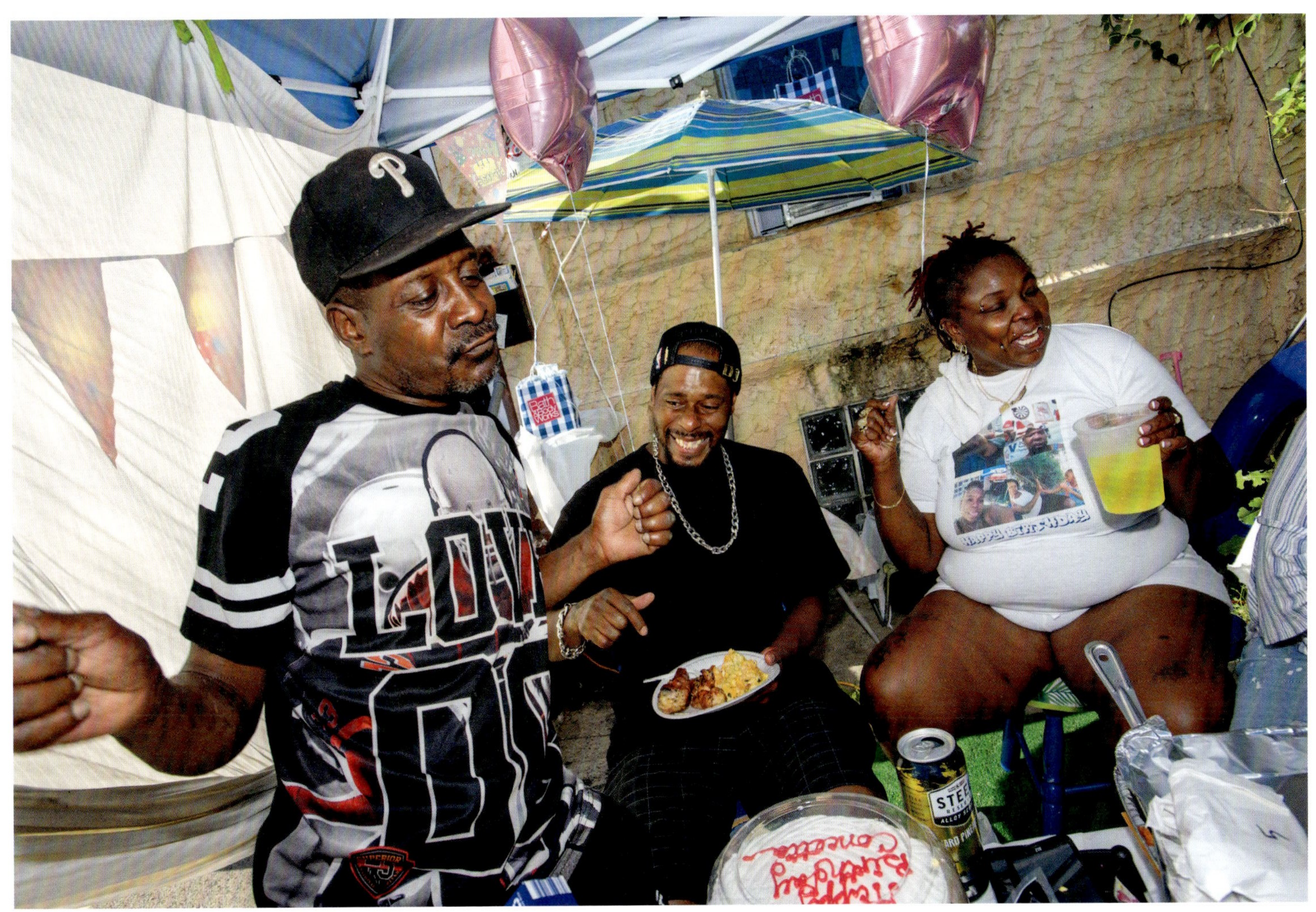

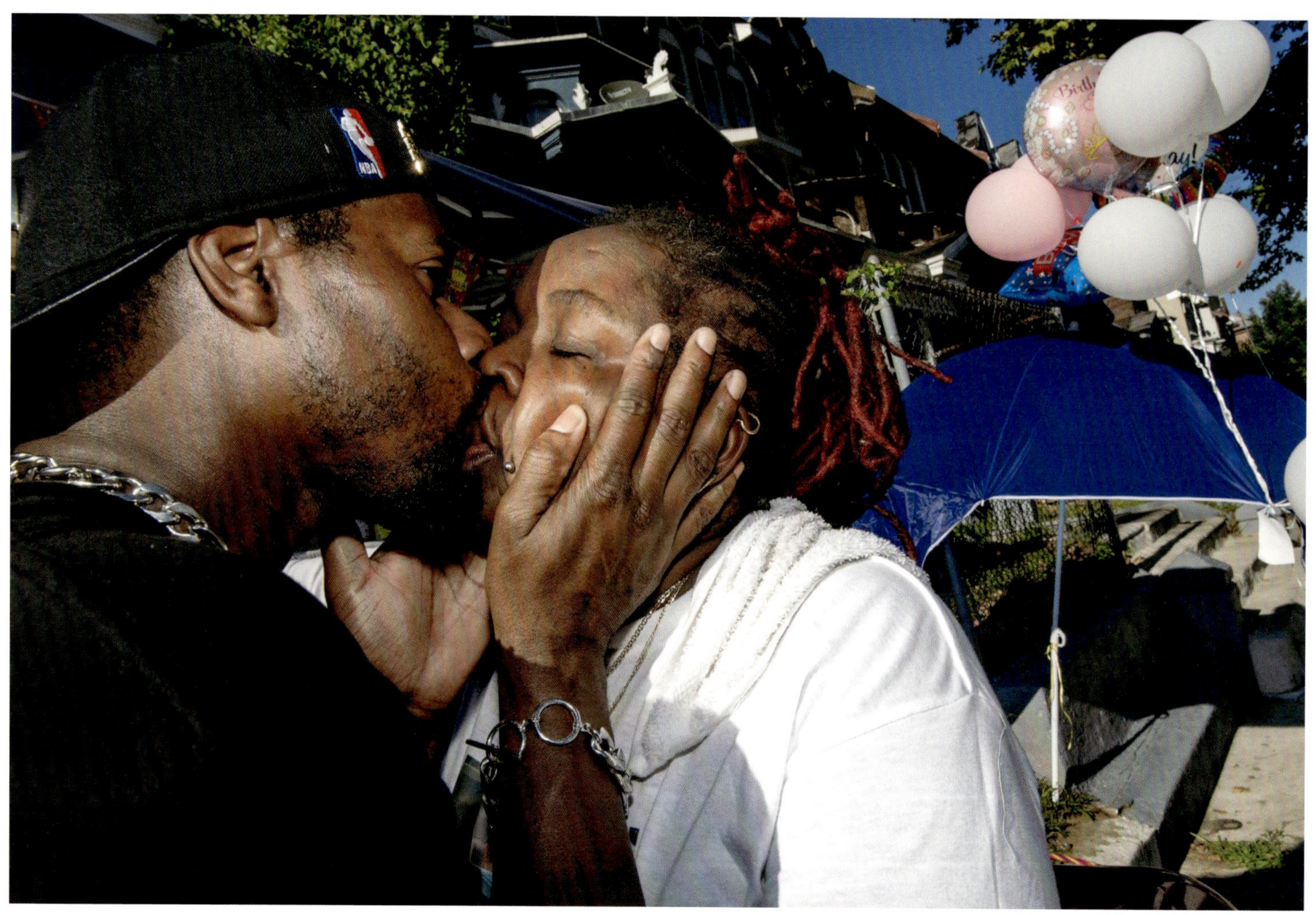

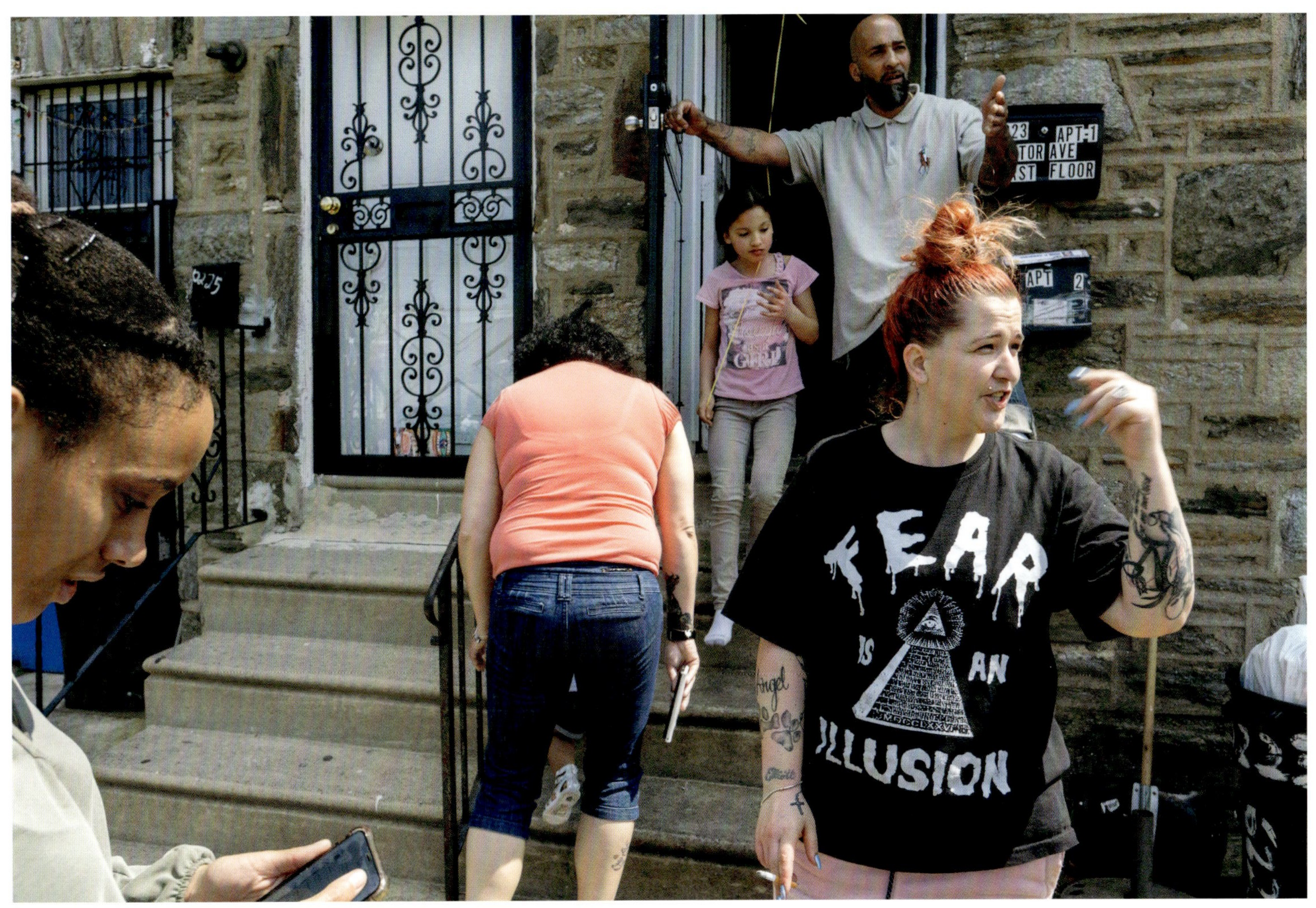
FEAR
IS AN
ILLUSION
23 APT-1
TOR AVE
ST FLOOR
APT 2

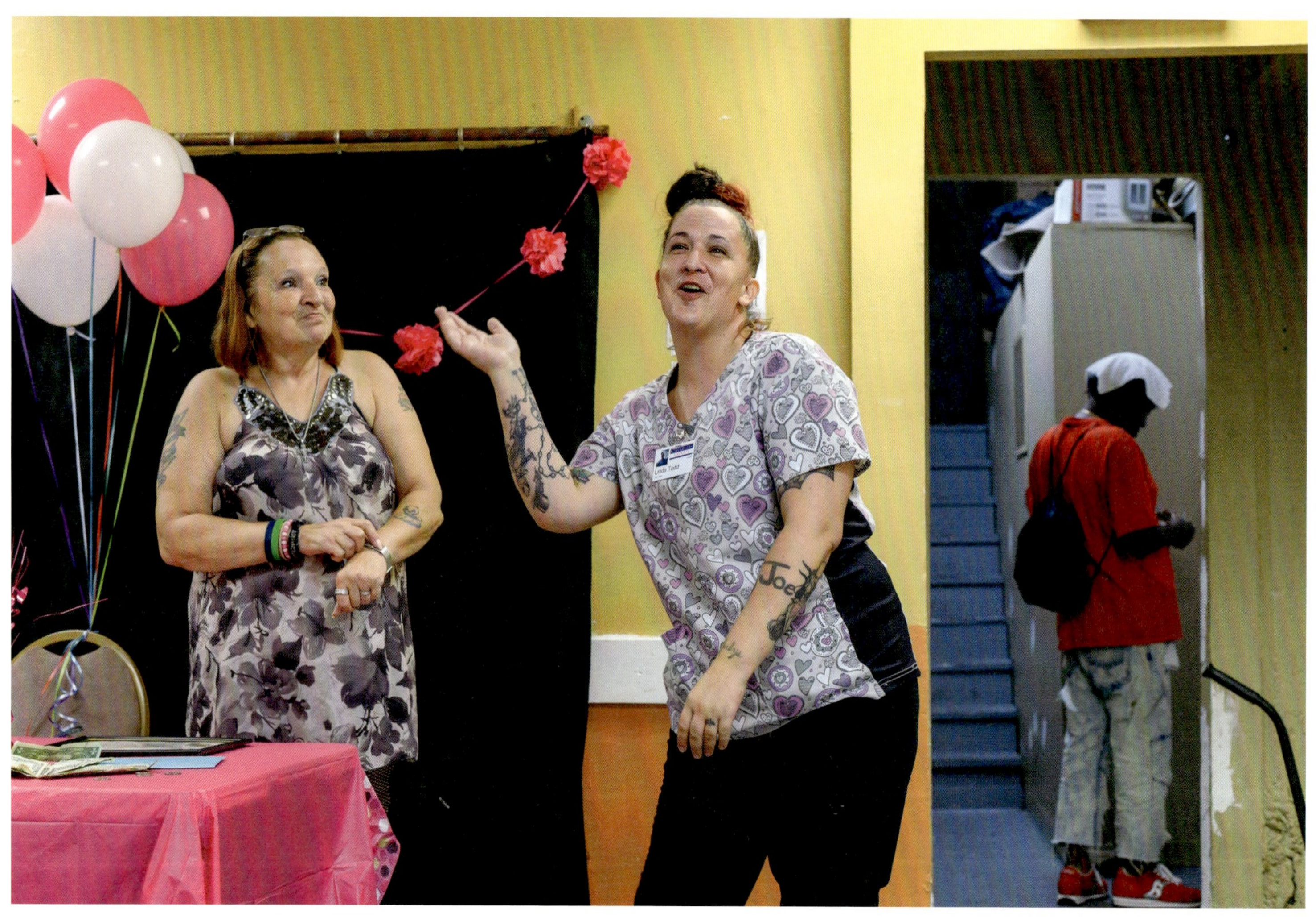

Maryann, Linda's mother, at the celebration of her first year of sobriety.

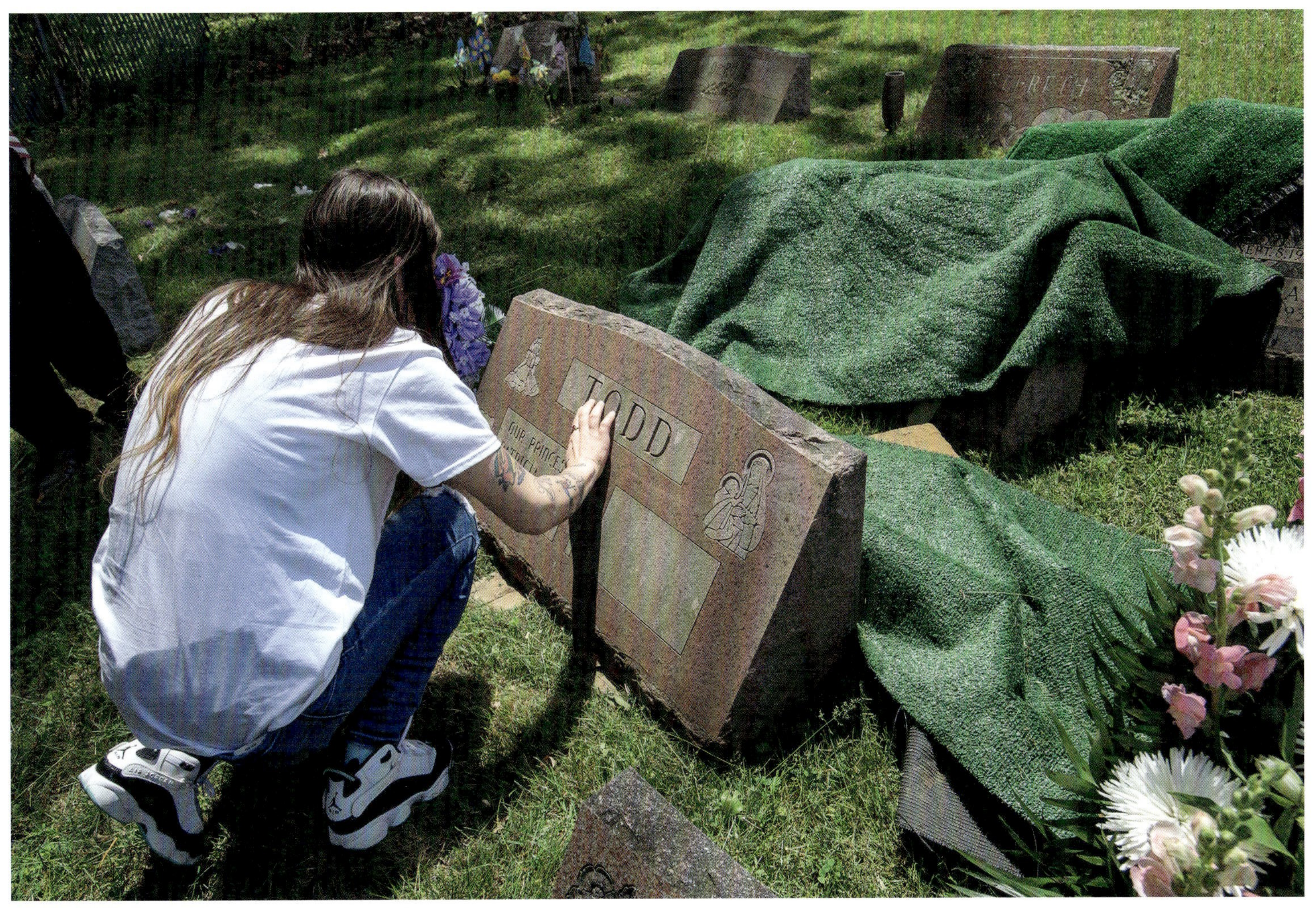

In May of 2022, Linda's mother, Maryann, died in her sleep and was buried next to a daughter, Patricia, who died in a tragic fire at a young age. Linda reaches out to touch the headstone of her sister.

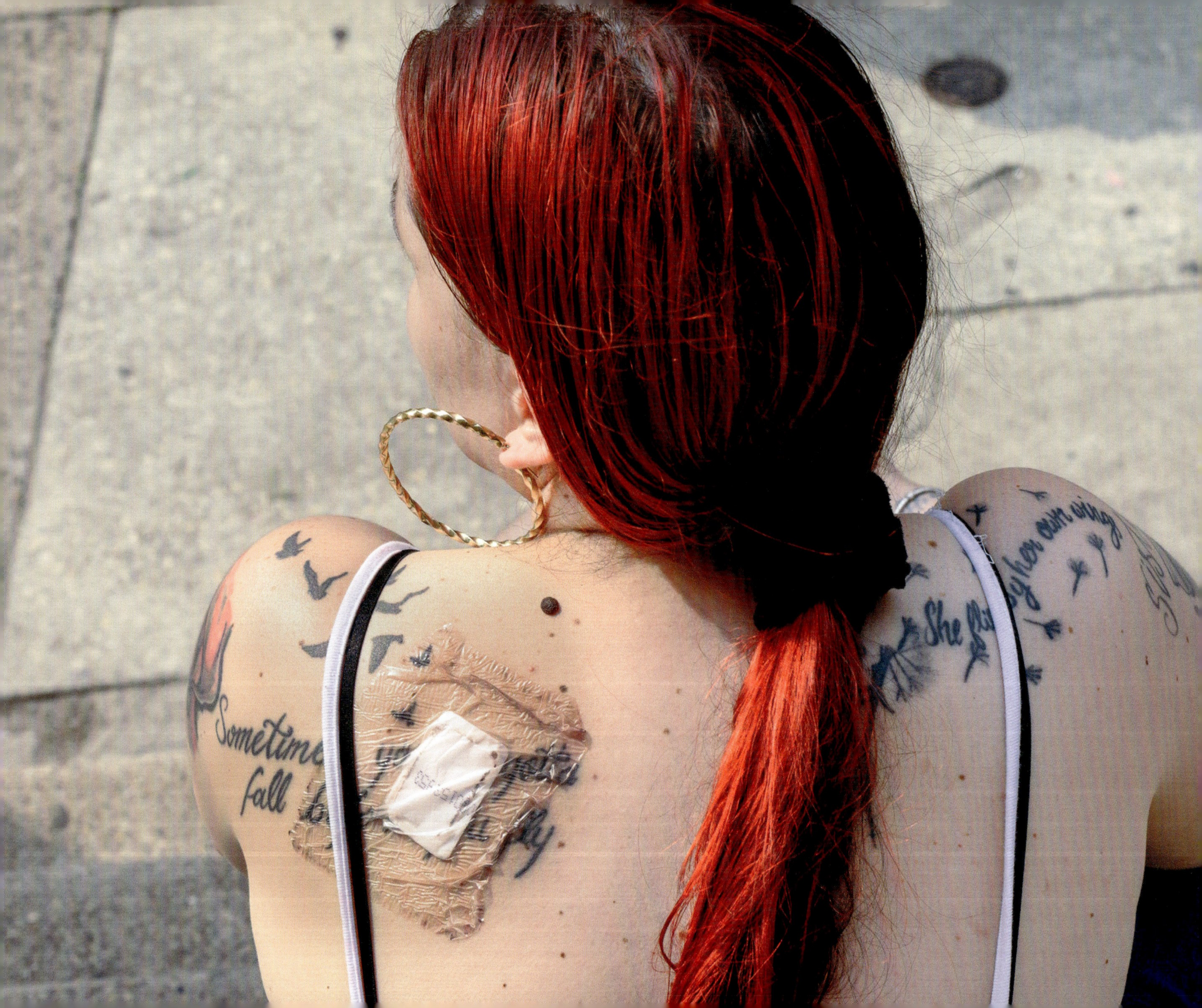
Sometimes
fall

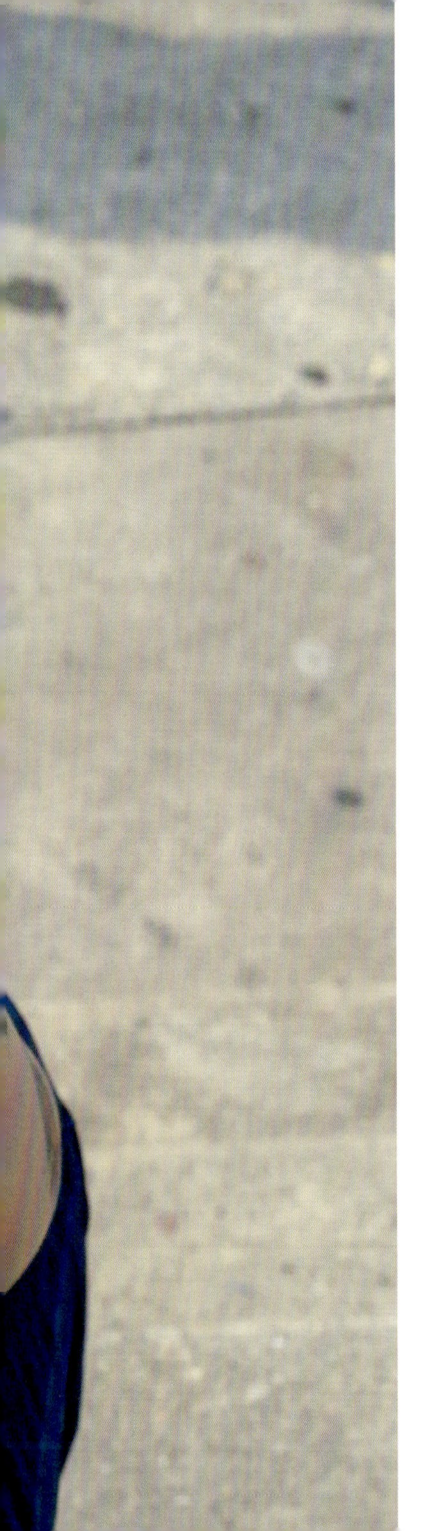

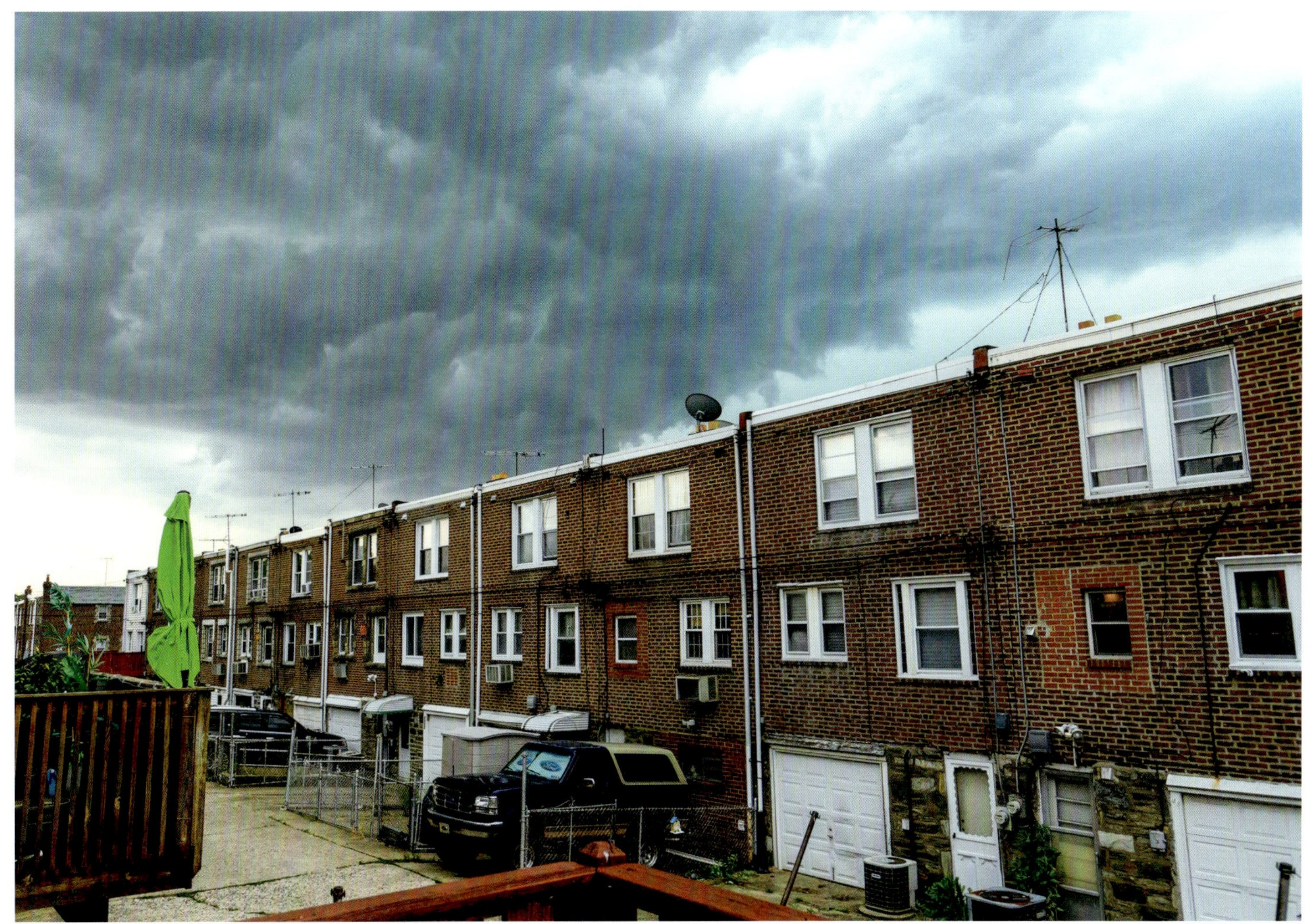

CAPTIONS

p. 16

Adriana can't wait for this pregnancy to be over. Her daughter, Brielle, does homework on Concetta's couch.

p. 18–20

The corner of Germantown Avenue and Butler Street, also just called "the corner." There is a laundromat, a deli across the street, a pizza place down the block, and the Nicetown Library on the same block. One can buy shots or beers at the deli and set up on the street in front of the laundromat to enjoy an afternoon. Roxy got a black eye when she was robbed here. She sits doing word puzzles while her laundry spins.

p. 22

Near the corner of Kensington and Allegheny Avenues some bad drugs hit the streets, causing massive overdoses all at once. The ambulances were zigzagging around trying to keep up. This intersection, where Linda worked at the K&A Diner, is the epicenter of the opioid drug crisis in Philadelphia. It also has the largest share of unhoused people in Philadelphia. It is known for gun violence, and mass transit stations used as bedrooms, bathrooms, and shooting galleries.

p. 26

A birthday party for Matt, Linda's half brother, held at the home Linda shares with Karlos. It is Matt's first birthday out of prison in many years.

p. 30

Kareem and Concetta wait for a ride in front of her house.

p. 31

Linda, at work as a home health aide. Her client is Damian's grandmother. She prepares breakfast for Damian, because she has offered to.

p. 34

Concetta, in green, kisses her grandson Bryce. Her granddaughter swings on the railing while Concetta's daughter, Adriana, sits on the stoop behind Concetta.

p. 43

Catherine, or Mom-Mom, staying home with grandson Kareem, who isn't feeling well. Catherine is Linda's stepmother and gave her a place to live when she was released from prison. This home is a few blocks from Kensington and Allegheny Avenues, one of the largest illegal drug markets on the East Coast.

p. 47

At a housewarming for Linda's sister, Dina, Linda needs to clear the air with her stepmother, Catherine (pink top), and her mother, Maryann (blue top, seated).

p. 54

Linda hugs Jenna at a memorial for Jenna's son Damian. Damian died of SIDS at the age of four months.

p. 57

Concetta isn't happy with me for taking photos while she rolls a joint. At the time of the photo, marijuana hadn't been made legal for personal use. Batman, however, in the black T-shirt, told her, "You know she's always got that camera."

p. 70

Jenna and Damian visit Linda at the diner. This is the last photograph ever made of Damian. He died that same week.

p. 74

Concetta prepares Thanksgiving in her very small kitchen. She manages to turn out turkey, mac and cheese, and green bean casserole.

p. 80

Linda, seated right; her sister, Dina, standing left; and their mother, Maryann, standing to the rear. The family is gathered for Dina's housewarming party.

p. 93

Concetta was shopping for diapers for her grandson when Adriana called with the panic of a woman who was in a very bad situation with her partner at the time.

p. 99

Linda sits on the step of the K&A Diner where she works. Her brother, Joe Bear, and mother, Maryann, had come for a visit. They weren't doing so well at the time. Her mother had been clean for five years when she passed away suddenly in the middle of the night in May 2022. Her brother, Joe, is clean now, and working and living close to Linda.

p. 100

A celebration of the life of Green Eyes, an unhoused man who sold goods up at the corner, and a friend of Concetta's. Everyone at the barbecue wore green to honor him. He was the victim of a hit-and-run accident caused by an off-duty police officer.

AFTERWORD

Amy Fettig, Executive Director, The Sentencing Project

Some of the most overlooked and vulnerable women in American society are in prisons and jails. And their numbers have been growing for decades, at rates twice as high as those for men. On any given day, over 200,000 women are incarcerated in a US prison or jail. This represents a 700 percent increase since 1980. It also means that the United States imprisons more women than any other country on the planet. In fact, while only 5 percent of the world's female population lives in the U.S., our country accounts for nearly 30 percent of the world's incarcerated women.

This is a stunning and devastating statistic. But it does not tell the full story of the women who are impacted, their children, families, and communities, or the collective failures of American society and our institutions that have turned this country into the world's greatest jailer of women.

The statistics don't tell the story of the children denied their mothers—as the vast majority of women in prisons and jails are custodial parents. The numbers also don't tell the story of the physical and sexual abuse and unaddressed trauma that characterize the lives of most women before they get caught up in our criminal legal system. Nor do they express the overwhelming level of untreated mental illness and substance abuse disorder that create direct pathways to prison for women in America. The numbers certainly don't reveal the devastated communities, where deliberate disinvestment in education, housing, health care, employment, and the social safety net funnels women, and especially women of color, into prisons and jails.

The statistics don't tell the full truth about the racism in America that underpins every aspect of our criminal legal system—even though we know that Black women are nearly twice as likely to be imprisoned as their white peers and Latinx women are 1.3 times more likely.

Importantly, the numbers also don't tell us about the struggle women face when they try to return home to their children and communities from prison or jail. They don't tell us about the lack of support for women trying to get housing, reunite with their children, support their families, obtain jobs, or even get something as basic as food stamps, menstrual products, transportation, or a prescription for life-saving medications.

The numbers don't tell us the full story, but women—in their own voices, in their own homes and communities—tell us what's really going on. They tell us about the struggle and the resilience it takes to survive our incarceration nation, and even to thrive, despite the barriers our society creates for its own people. The women we meet in *Done Doing Time* have a lot to say and a lot to teach all of us. They give us the gift of seeing their harsh realities and their hard-won triumphs. Through their example we can learn to be a better country, a better community, and better neighbors to all. But first, we need to start listening, looking, and learning more from the women who know this world best.

ACKNOWLEDGMENTS

Magdalena Solé deserves more than an acknowledgment for her support, wisdom, and sensibilities in bringing this book to fruition. Her encouragement kept me going through the years.

My wife, Susan Toler, has supported and encouraged me from the very beginning and has not let her enthusiasm waiver. Her love, patience, and humor are with me every day.

To all the women in Magdalena's book-editing workshop, which took place in the depths of the Covid pandemic, I so appreciate your support and thoughtfulness. Adele Epstein, Elizabeth Guseman, Ewa Zebrowski, Gaye Leggat, Loli Kantor, and Sally Thomson. Thank you all.

BIOGRAPHY

Hinda Schuman is a documentary photographer, photojournalist, and educator. She spent twenty years at the *Philadelphia Inquirer* covering regional news and sports. Prior to her career at the *Inquirer*, she taught reading and other subjects to students in grades one through eight in Vermont. Hinda was the volunteer coordinator for the Brattleboro (VT) Area Women's Crisis Center, assisting women who were fleeing their abusers. She also worked as a counselor at a group home, baked bread in a factory, and built two houses from foundation to roof. After getting her MFA from Tyler School of Art and Architecture in 1985, she installed door knockers in an apartment building. A wonderful meeting with a photography editor at the *Philadelphia Inquirer* led to her full-time position as a photojournalist. Her first book, *Dear Shirley*, was published by Daylight Books in 2018.

Hinda was born in Brooklyn, NY, in 1948, and now lives in Philadelphia, PA, with her wife, Susan. They have three fabulous grandchildren.